GW01605578

CARY GRANT

CARY GRANT

IN THE SPOTLIGHT

GALLEY PRESS
A Division of Mayflower Books, Inc.
New York, New York 10022

Manufactured in the United States of America.
First American Edition.

ISBN: 8317—3957—6

Library of Congress Catalog Card Number: 80-82357

PHOTO CREDITS

Hy Simon Archive
11, 64, 121 (top), 136

Museum of Modern Art/Film Stills Archive
8 (bottom), 12, 14-15, 18, 19 (left), 25, 28-29, 31, 33, 35, 36, 37, 38-39, 40, 41, 45, 46, 47, 49, 50-51, 52, 53, 55, 56, 58-59, 61, 62, 63, 65, 67, 70, 71, 72, 73, 76-77, 78, 79, 80, 81, 83, 84, 87, 88-89, 90, 94, 105, 106, 107, 111, 120, 121 (bottom), 122, 123 (bottom), 124, 125 (top), 126 (top & bottom), 127, 128 (top & bottom), 129 (top & bottom), 130 (top & bottom), 131, 132 (top), 133 (top), 134 (top & bottom), 137 (top & bottom), 138 (top & bottom), 139, 140, 141 (top & bottom), 142, 143 (left & right), 144 (top left & top right, bottom), 145, 146 (top & bottom), 147, 148 (top & bottom), 149, 150 (top & bottom), 151, 152 (top & bottom), 153, 154 (top & bottom), 155 (top & bottom), 156, 157 (top & bottom), 158 (top & bottom), 159 (top & bottom), 160 (top left & bottom left, right).

UPI
7, 8 (top), 9, 10, 13, 16, 17, 19 (right), 20, 21, 22, 23, 24, 26, 27, 32, 34, 42-43, 48, 57, 60 (left & right), 66-67, 68, 74, 75, 82, 85, 86, 91, 93, 95, 96-97, 98, 99, 100, 101 (left & right), 102-103, 104, 108-109, 110, 112, 113, 114, 115, 116-117, 125 (bottom), 135.

Title page photograph: UPI

CONTENTS

1 CARY GRANT:

HOLLYWOOD'S PERFECT LEADING MAN

Cary Grant:

Hollywood's Perfect Leading Man

Cary Grant made his first motion picture in 1932, at age twenty-eight; his last in 1966, when he was sixty-six years old. Between these years, during a career encompassing seventy-two films, he developed the unique character and charm his audience came to anticipate and enjoy—a character caught in varied circumstances, but, with few exceptions, dependably predictable.

Grant once said of himself: "When I appear on the screen, I'm playing myself. It's harder to play yourself. I pretended to be a certain kind of man on screen, and I became that man in life. I became me. But to play yourself—your true self—is the hardest thing in the world to do. Watch people at a party. They're playing themselves like everything—but nine times out of ten the image of themselves they adopt is the wrong one. Adopt the true image of yourself, acquire a technique to project it, and the public will give you its allegiance."

This has been Cary Grant's success formula. Other actors may attempt elaborate method techniques, develop ability and versatility in characterization, but Grant knew during his film career what he could do best, and on this he capitalized. He is, he readily admits, not an actor of great range, but of all the tall, dark, and handsome actors to appear on screen, Cary Grant is the epitome. Of every other smooth, dashing, leading man, it might fairly be said: "He's good, but he's no Cary Grant."

Cary Grant is best known as *the* prototypical leading man of light comedy; however, he was also a dramatic actor of great power. In *Gunga Din* (1939) and *Destination Tokyo* (1944), he extended his performing range to include the action hero genre. In a 1944 release, *None But the Lonely Heart,* he played a poor criminal trying to break free of his life outside the law. The Cary Grant the world came to know best,

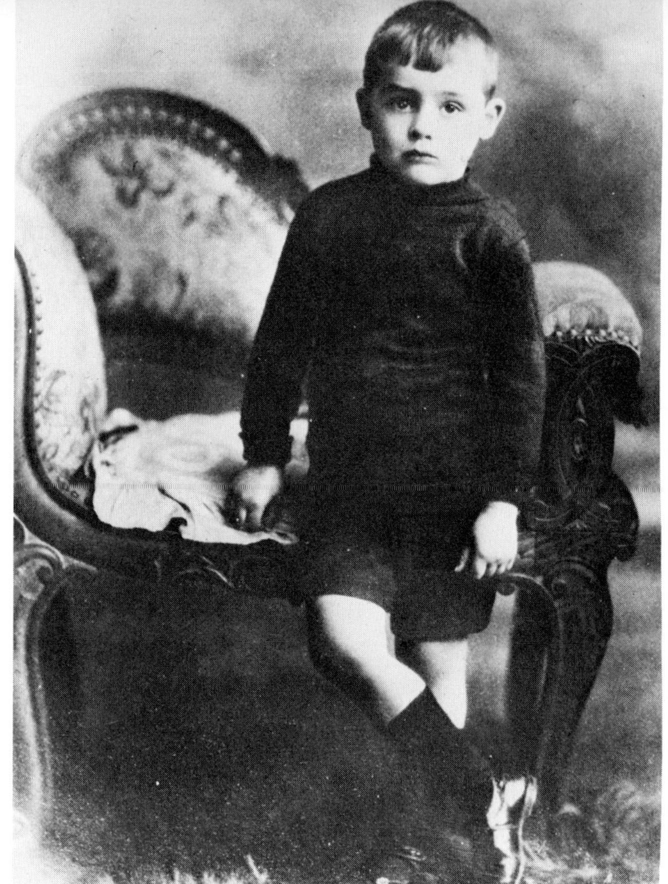

Archie Leach (Cary Grant), about 1910.

(Right) On the run at the Paramount lot, 1932.

Members of the Bob Pender Troupe, with Pender seated, flanked (l.) by his wife and (r.) his daughter.

(Left) At lunch, still wearing makeup, at the Paramount commissary with novelist Tiffany Thayer (r.), 1932.

(Above) With Sylvia Sidney and Charles Ruggles in a scene from *Madame Butterfly* (1932).

though, was the self-effacing romantic and comedic lead who added a certain grace and charm, even to awkward moments, in every film in which he appeared. These are the qualities that the words "Cary Grant" have come to represent to generations of film fans.

Cary Grant was born Archibald Leach on January 18, 1904, in Bristol, England, a seaport city located southwest of London. His parents were middle-class Episcopalians. Elias James Leach, his father, who worked for a textile firm, was adored by his son. "He was a dear, sweet man and I learned a lot from him. He first put into my mind the idea of buying one superior suit rather than a number of inferior ones. Then even when it's threadbare, people will know it

Listening to fellow actor Richard Arlen (l.) on the Paramount lot, 1932.

was once good. He taught me the feel of good cloth and a liking for expensive shoes. I've paid $150 for a pair of shoes. They look better even after years of wear. I've always believed that it's good sense to pay a lot."

Archie was not the first born. Some years before his birth, his mother, Elsie Kingdom Leach, lost a two-month-old boy to convulsions. The child had been ill for days, and a doctor at last ordered Mrs. Leach to get some sleep. When she awakened, her baby was dead.

In 1913, when Archie was nine years old, Elsie suffered a nervous breakdown and was institutionalized. Archie would not see his mother again for many years. Her absence was perceived by the young boy as a willful, unexplained disappearance.

That same year, Archie discovered the Bristol Hippodrome, where he became fascinated with entertainers whose antics and life styles were so totally foreign to him. "I found my inarticulate self in a dazzling land of smiling, jostling people. They were wearing, and not wearing, all sorts of costumes and doing all sorts of clever things. And that's when I knew. What other life could there be but that of an actor?"

In 1916, when Archie was twelve years old, he accepted (unbeknownst to his father) a part in a traveling company of youngsters; but Mr. Leach had the authorities retrieve Archie, and he was made to endure more formal education. Archie's ambitions simmered for four years until he joined the Bob Pender troupe of acrobats. This time, Mr. Leach reasoned that his son was old enough to know his own mind and did not attempt to interfere.

In 1920, the Pender troupe traveled to New York. When they returned to England, Archie was not among them. He remained in the United States in hope of developing a talent for song and dance. "Looking back, I consider that making the jump from acrobatics was the greatest hurdle of all. As in pictures, vaudeville people are classified and expected to keep within those limits."

At age seventeen, Archie found the going tough. He made the rounds of booking offices, finding no one interested in helping him. When his savings were exhausted, he sought shelter with friends and slept on park benches and in deserted office buildings. Finally, he found a job: a stilt walker advertising Tilyou's Steeplechase Park on the boardwalk of Coney Island. Another job was selling hand-painted neckties created by his artist friend, John (Orry) Kelly (who later would win an Oscar for costume design for *An American in Paris*). Eventually, Archie organized a small acting troupe made up of some of the entertainers that he had met in New York. He did make some money with the troupe; as a solo performer, however, Archie soon realized that he needed more training before he could assault the Great White Way with any authority. "I decided that I must get more experience as an actor and then come back and conquer Broadway. I was discouraged but not defeated. I felt confident that I would again have an opportunity and when it came along, I wanted to be prepared."

On a tea break at the Paramount commissary with visitors Russell Clark (r.), president of the New Orleans Cotton Exchange, and Clark's wife, 1932.

So, Grant went back to England and worked with the Nightingale Stock Company his first season back there. As luck would have it, present for one of his performances was Reggie Hammerstein, a producer from New York, who offered Archie a theatrical contract which included a role in *Polly,* a musical to be performed in the United States. Archie re-

With co-star Marlene Dietrich in Blonde Venus (1932).

Grant and actor Randolph Scott (l.), a close friend, were born 5 days apart: Nancy Carroll (c.) surprised them both with a chocolate cake on the Paramount lot, 1933.

turned to New York (this time with a coveted contract), where he played in *Golden Dawn* (1927) while *Polly's* opening was delayed. *Golden Dawn* ran for 184 performances. Archie then joined the cast of *Polly,* but the show flopped in its tryout. The exposure helped: a Shubert scout noticed Archie and later bought his contract from Hammerstein.

Archie was soon signed to play the lead opposite Jeanette MacDonald in *Boom, Boom* (1929). The show had a long run on Broadway, allowing Archie Leach to make his first lasting

Grant and Randolph Scott rush Virginia Cherrill toward a cafe on the Paramount set. Cherrill had won acclaim as Charlie Chaplin's leading lady in *City Lights* (1931).

Recalling his vaudeville days, Grant does a balancing act.

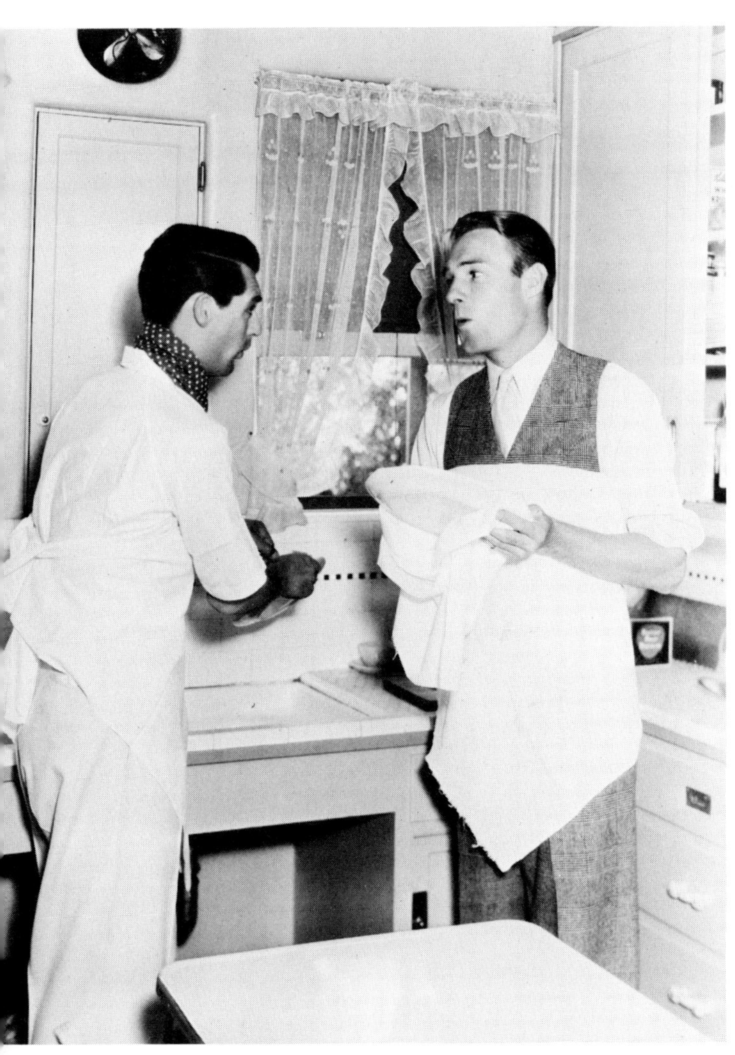

Housekeeping with pal Randolph Scott, 1933.

Grant and Lona Andre, another Paramount player, ride a midget car on the set of *The Woman Accused* (1933).

impression and his first weighty paycheck: $450 a week for the run of the show.

His next engagement on Broadway was in the play *Nikki* (1931), in which Archie played a character named Cary Lockwood. Co-starring were Fay Wray and Douglas Montgomery. The show lasted only thirty-nine performances.

Archie decided to leave New York to pursue a film career in California. Director and friend Marion Gering was making a screen test of a young actress and Archie was asked to help in the reading of the script. Ironically, it was Archie who was signed, not the girl.

Now a Paramount Pictures property, Archie set about developing a character that would be able to withstand constant exposure. "The tough thing, the final thing, is to be yourself. That takes doing and I should know. I used to [imitate] Noel Coward. Hand plunged in the pocket, you know. It took me three long years to get my silly hand out of there, and they were three years wasted. Noel Coward is great at being Noel Coward; the role I do best is [me]."

Vacationing with Virginia Cherrill at the Desert Inn, Palm Springs, CA, 1933.

As a member of the Paramount family, Archie was asked to select a new name. "I liked my original name. But Paramount was paying me and they didn't like it. Cary was the name of the character I'd played in my last New York show. I took a pin to a list of last names and came up with Grant. At first it seemed odd to change my name, but I really didn't mind."

During this period, Archie appeared in *Singapore Sue,* a ten-minute musical short. Writer-director Casey Robinson reminisced: "I needed a leading man to play an American sailor. Among the young men brought to see me was Archie Leach, who had never been in front of a camera. I liked him and cast him without hesitation. This young actor, Archie, so impressed me during the filming that I wrote a note to important executives at Paramount, none of whom I knew at the time, urging them to screen the short, not for my work, but for that of a young actor whom I felt to be a sure-fire future star."

By the time *Singapore Sue* appeared, Archie Leach had become Cary Grant and was filming *This Is the Night* (1932) with Thelma Todd, Roland Young, Lily Damita, and Charles Ruggles. In this, his first full-length film, Grant plays an Olympic javelin thrower. Thelma Todd, as his wife, attracts the attention of Roland Young. Grant, in turn, becomes infatuated with Damita, who is Young's wife.

The major studios got plenty of mileage out of their actors in the Thirties, and Grant appeared in seven motion pictures during the first year of his contract.

Grant's second picture, *Sinners in the Sun* (1932), was a Carole Lombard vehicle. Lombard plays an ambitious New York City working woman who leaves her job for Long Island's high society, only to discover at last that the path to happiness requires love, not merely money and affairs. One of those affairs was with Grant. His brief appearance received little notice.

Next in line was *Merrily We Go to Hell* (1932). Sylvia Sidney and Fredric March play an unstable heiress-writer couple, and Grant is seen briefly as an actor in one of playwright

At a party in the Club New Yorker, Hollywood, with Virginia Cherrill, soon after the couple formalized their engagement. French-Canadian actress Fifi Dorsay (c.) holds the plate.

March's productions.

Devil and the Deep (1932), Grant's fourth film, was directed by Marion Gering, the man who signed Grant to his Paramount contract. In *Devil and the Deep,* Grant appears in the film's first half hour only, playing Lieutenant Jaeckel, a young officer stationed on a submarine. Charles Laughton is the sub's Commander Sturm; he's married to Tallulah Bankhead and rightfully suspects there is an affair between her and Jaeckel. Replacing the handsome lieutenant (deliberately transferred by Sturm), is a character played by Gary Cooper who proves to be more of a threat to Sturm than Jaeckel was.

Blonde Venus (1932) was Grant's next picture. The film was one of seven soft-focus melodramas starring Marlene Dietrich and directed by Josef von Sternberg. It received unfavorable reviews. Grant's showing, however, impressed Paramount, and when Gary Cooper turned down roles in *Hot Saturday* (1932) and *Madame Butterfly* (1932), Grant was called upon.

Hot Saturday, a story of love and jealousy, co-stars Nancy Carroll: Grant plays a wealthy Beau Brummell who returns Miss Carroll to her home at an indecent hour after a party, whereupon Randolph Scott, playing her fiance, breaks off their engagement. Furious, Carroll runs to Grant to make true what others had wrongfully suspected her of. In the final scene, Grant and Carroll drive off, presumably to seek a justice of the peace. *Hot Saturday* was Grant's first leading role and the consensus was that he showed promise. At age twenty-eight, he was a rising star in Hollywood.

Grant also developed some personal relationships during this period. His closest friend was Randolph Scott, with whom he shared a bungalow and the experiences of bachelor life. It was during this time that Grant gained a reputation for being stingy. "I'm sure I have that reputation because I don't gamble or go to nightclubs or give huge parties. And I don't believe in giving gifts at Christmas, either. I give presents when I feel like it." Carole Lombard once said of Scott and Grant's bill-paying pro-

(Left) Dancing with Virginia Cherrill at the Club New Yorker, a favorite Hollywood night spot, 1933.

(Above) Grant and Virginia Cherrill outside the Register Office, London, minutes after their marriage, Feb. 15, 1934.

cedure: "Cary opened the bills, Randy wrote the checks, and if Cary could talk someone out of some postage stamps, he mailed them."

Randolph Scott always had praise ready for his close friend and roommate and once told an interviewer: "He's easy to live with, considerate of others, doesn't interfere or try to give advice however well meant, has the courage to fight for his convictions, is a graceful winner and a good loser, never out-fumbles in doing his share, and has a punchy sense of humor."

During a radio interview in L.A., 1933. Morton Downey (r.), radio star, and Eleanor Barnes, newspaper dramatic editor, attend.

Grant and Scott occasionally gave small parties, and it was at one of these parties that Grant met the young actress Virginia Cherrill and, as he recalls, "I fell in love with her almost the minute she walked in."

Miss Cherrill was born on a farm in Carthage, Illinois. While visiting a friend on the West Coast (Sue Carol, later to marry Alan Ladd), Virginia met Charlie Chaplin, who asked her to take a screen test. She consented, and although she had never before acted, she was cast in *City Lights*. She and Grant began to see each other whenever their schedules permitted.

Madame Butterfly was Grant's final picture of 1932. In Hollywood's dramatic interpretation of Giacomo Puccini's opera, Grant plays Lieutenant Pinkerton; Sylvia Sidney plays Cho-cho San, the geisha who falls in love with him while he's stationed in Yokohama.

The Grant speaking voice and manner was fast becoming a distinctive trademark; Grant impressed the ladies in his naval garb in *Madame Butterfly,* and Mae West, also impressed, cast him opposite herself in *She Done Him Wrong* (1933). In this story of The Bowery in New York in the 1890s, Mae West plays Lou, a saloon entertainer and girlfriend of Gus Jordon (Noah Beery, Sr.). Jordan operates a dance hall, a white slave ring, and a counterfeiting business. Lou becomes attracted to Grant, a federal agent posing as a Salvation Army administrator, and eventually the two of them put Jordan away. Of Mae West, Grant later commented:

Publicity pose, 1934.

Two glimpses into the home of Cary Grant and his wife Virginia Cherrill, 1934.

"I learned everything from her. Well, not everything, but almost everything. She knows so much. Her instinct is so true, her timing so perfect, her grasp of the situation so right."

The ninth film of Grant's career was *The Woman Accused* (1933), a shipboard murder story adapted for the screen by Bayard Veiller from a *Liberty Magazine* fiction series. Nancy Carroll co-starred.

The Eagle and the Hawk (1933) concerns itself with the World War I Royal Flying Corps. Grant appears along with Fredric March; the two portray flying aces. On the ground, they are enemies, but in the air, they work as a team. The film co-stars Carole Lombard as March's girlfriend. The love scenes, the airborne fighting sequences, and the pilots' character development provided enough box-office pull to make the picture a success.

Grant's fourth film of 1933 was *Gambling Ship,* a romance between a young, handsome gangster (Grant) and the mistress of a shipping magnate (Benita Hume). Neither lover knows the other's background, providing some sus-

pense in *Gambling Ship.*

In *I'm No Angel* (1933), Grant's next film, Mae West confidently chose Grant to star opposite her for the second time in the same year. She and Grant act with great effect; West as a lion tamer named Tira, Grant as the rich playboy Jack Clayton. The couple are attracted to each other from the start. *I'm No Angel* contains some of Mae West's finest lines: "Beulah, peel me a grape." "When I'm good, I'm very good. But when I'm bad, I'm better." Wesley Ruggles (an original Keystone Kop) directed.

Closing out 1933 for Grant was director Norman Z. McLeod's *Alice in Wonderland.* This screen adaptation, Hollywood's most original interpretation of Lewis Carroll's classic, features Grant in the part of the Mock Turtle, W. C. Fields as Humpty Dumpty, and Charles Ruggles as the March Hare.

Throughout 1933, Grant's romance with actress Virginia Cherrill flourished. The *New Movie Magazine* of March, 1934, printed the following in an article on Grant: "Of course, as everyone knows, Cary really admires only one

With wife Virginia Cherrill at the Brown Derby, L.A., 1934.

girl and that is the charming blonde, Virginia Cherrill. About their romance he has little to say, although if they are Mr. and Mrs. by the time this article appears, I shouldn't be the least surprised . . . Right now the world is at his feet. It's great to be young, successful and in love!"

On February 9, 1934, Grant and Cherrill had in fact been married in London, but by September of that same year, the tensions of marriage and careers had become severe enough for Miss Cherrill to leave Grant for her mother's house. "I'm still in love with Cary and I hope and feel certain that we will be able to patch things up and continue with our marriage," she said at the time. Grant was distraught: "It's silly to say Virginia and I have separated. We have just had a quarrel, such as any married couple might have. I hope when I get home tonight, Virginia will be waiting for me."

On October 5, 1934, Grant made national headlines when he was rushed unconscious to a hospital. Cherrill ran to his side; after learning, however, that he had simply passed out from too much alcohol and would be well in a day, she returned to her mother's. Grant later explained: "You know what whiskey does when you drink it all by yourself. It makes you very, very sad. I began calling people up." He also revealed: "I know I called Virginia. I don't remember what I said to her, but things got hazier and hazier. I'd sure hate to leave this world. It would be a much better one if Virginia would come back, though. I'm ashamed of getting drunk."

His explanations had no effect on Virginia. She filed a maintenance suit claiming Grant had not sent her a penny since their separation. Grant was ordered to pay $167.50 a week until a divorce trail was held.

On March 26, 1935, Cherrill was granted a divorce, and Grant returned to Randolph Scott's Malibu bungalow alone and depressed. For a time, he dated Ginger Rogers and Mary Brian. "But I don't go out nearly as much as the columnists claim. I never did. The only reason I get in the papers so often is because I'm a so-called 'eligible bachelor.' There are only a few of the species left, so the columnists have to use the names over and over, whether you were actually out nightclubbing or not. There's no fun in reporting married couples out with each other. There's no scandal in that."

Grant has always been a complicated person and this apparently caused conflict in his relationships with women. Years later, friend Clifford Odets remarked about Grant: "His simplicity covers up one of the most complex people I've ever met. After sixteen years I sometimes feel as if I really don't know him at all." Director Leo McCarey: "He's extremely bright, intriguing and interesting. But after all these years, I still don't know what makes him tick." Late in his career, Grant himself commented on his youth: "I was an utter fake, a self-opinionated boor, hiding behind all kinds of defenses, hypocrisies and vanities. I had to get rid of them layer by layer."

Grant has often been preoccupied with self-doubt. *McCall's* in September, 1958, wrote: ". . . he wears different hats when he's with different people. Depending on who you are, you'll see him wear his Glamorous Movie Star hat, his Health hat, his Agonized Actor hat, his Get Your Money's Worth hat, his Interior Decorator's hat — or any number of others." "He is a disturbed man," said one director. "Of the sixteen hours a day that he's awake, I don't think there are twenty minutes when he's not complaining. I've never seen a man more constantly in turmoil."

Divorced and single again in Hollywood, Grant, nonetheless, proceeded undauntedly with his career. *Thirty-Day Princess* (1934) reunited him with Sylvia Sidney, who plays an actress hired to impersonate the Princess of Taronia, a mythical European kingdom. Grant is a young newspaper executive reluctant to recommend passage of a huge loan for the princess's country, but he is persuaded by Sidney's royal charm and approves the loan.

In 1934, Grant and Loretta Young filmed *Born to Be Bad* for Darryl F. Zanuck at Twentieth Century pictures. It is a melodrama concerning the battle of an unwed mother (Loretta Young) to acquire her son from his adoptive

Having his picture taken with canine star "Squeezit," mid-1930s.

Irene Castle McLaughlin, stage and screen dancing star, lunches with Grant and actor Edward Everett Horton (r.) at the Paramount lot, 1934.

parents.

He then appeared in two films in rapid succession for Paramount. They were *Kiss and Make-Up* (1934) and *Ladies Should Listen* (1934). In *Kiss and Make-Up,* Grant and Edward Everett Horton act amusingly camp in a story revolving around a Paris beauty salon that specializes in transforming homely women into stunning royalty. Grant falls in love with one of his creations (Genevieve Tobin). The movie "succeeds to a remarkable degree in being dull," said *The New York Times.*

Ladies Should Listen ran for only an hour, but the critics felt that was sufficient. *Variety* wrote: "Basically there may have been enough comedy and farce possibility in this story, but as handled, it emerges as a much too highly strained attempt at farce. A good deal of it is actually unfunny, and all of it is too synthetic." Ann Sheridan made one of her early appearances in this film.

Enter Madame (1934), released in January, 1935, concerns a young man's marriage to an operatic prima donna (Elissa Landi). Made to

With Claude Rains (l.) in *The Last Outpost* (1935).

endure dog walking chores and other insensitivities by his celebrity wife, Grant abandons her, finds another love, but eventually returns to his wife—with their marriage now made better by the trauma his departure caused.

Myrna Loy stars with Grant in *Wings in the Dark* (1935), a tale of unspoken love between a female stunt pilot (Loy) and flier-inventor Ken Gordon (Grant). Gordon, working on an improved cockpit instrumentation system and on the brink of success, is blinded by a gas explosion. Sheila (the stunt pilot) supports Ken with her hard-earned dollars, but soon pressed with overwhelming bills, she attempts a Moscow-to-New York flight to raise money. During the flight, Sheila runs into severe weather and begins floundering. Ken, with the help of his mechanic-friend, flies through a cloud covering and, using his latest inventions to battle the weather, guides Sheila to safety. During the landing, Ken declares his love for Sheila, and the end of the film implies a new beginning for both.

Grant's second and final picture of 1935 was *The Last Outpost,* co-starring Claude Rains and Gertrude Michael. Grant plays Michael Andrews, a British officer who must warn a defenseless tribe against a Kurd attack. A love triangle provides an equally strong source of interest. Andrews (Grant) is recuperating in a hospital and has an affair with his nurse, Rosemary Haydon (Michael). Claude Rains shows up to reclaim his estranged wife who, to no one's surprise, turns out to be the nurse. After

Costume party at the Vendome Cafe, Hollywood, mid-1930s. Left to right: Grant, actress Mary Pickford, Countess De Frasso, and Tullio Carminati.

three years apart, she refuses to return to her husband (a Kurd officer), and later, after a desert battle, Rains, dying in Grant's arms, asks Grant to take care of her.

A highlight of 1935 for Grant was his first appearance on the Lux Radio Theatre in the play *Adam and Eve*. He would later appear on the Lux program several more times and would also make guest radio appearances on such programs as Groucho Marx's Kellogg show, Eddie Cantor's show, and George Faulkner's "The Circle."

In 1936, Paramount loaned Grant to RKO to make a film with director George Cukor. Co-starring Katharine Hepburn, it offered Grant an opportunity to play a different type of role. "For once they didn't see me as a nice young man with regular features and a heart of gold." Said director Cukor of Grant's acting in *Sylvia Scarlett* (1936): "Up to then, he had been a rather handsome, rather wooden leading man. But suddenly, during the shooting, he felt all his talents coming into being—maybe because it was the first part which really suited his background. He suddenly burst into bloom. It produced a wonderful performance."

In the movie, Grant appears as Jimmy Monkley, a Cockney petty thief whom Hepburn and her father (Edmund Gwenn) join up with after they have fled France. Hepburn disguises herself as a boy, and they practice swindling in London. Eventually, they turn themselves into an acting troupe. Robert Landry in *Variety* said that Cary Grant "...practically steals the picture. This is especially true in the earlier sequences. A scene in an English mansion to which Miss Hepburn, Grant and Gwenn have gone for purposes of robbery is dominated by Grant."

Next, in 1936, came *Big Brown Eyes* in which Joan Bennett plays a hotel barbershop manicurist in love with detective Danny Barr (Grant). The film is part suspense, part wacky comedy.

That same year, Grant made *Suzy* with Jean Harlow and Franchot Tone. Harlow plays Suzy, an American showgirl in London in 1914 who marries Terry (Tone). Mistakenly believing that Terry has been killed by a spy, she flees to Paris, where she meets and soon marries Andre (Grant), a French aviator. Her first husband, Terry, comes to Paris, sees Suzy, but does not expose their previous marriage. Andre is then actually killed by a spy, and Suzy and Terry arrange to have Andre's death appear to be combat-related. With Andre hailed as a hero, the original couple renew their happy life together. Dorothy Parker contributed to the screenplay and some aerial footage by Howard Hughes was borrowed for authenticity.

At a Hollywood party. Toby Wing and Mitchell Leisen directly behind Grant; Cesar Romero second from top of slide.

Wedding Present (1936) concluded Grant's contract with Paramount. He plays an eccentric newspaperman, Charlie, who is thrust into an administrative position where his zany antics have much greater impact. He also loses the love and loyalty of Rusty (Joan Bennett), a

In conversation with actor Jack Oakie, 1936.

On location for *Suzy* (1936), with actress Benita Hume.

With (l. to r.) Dennie Moore, Katharine Hepburn, and Edmund Gwenn in *Sylvia Scarlett* (1936).

Publicity photograph, *The Awful Truth* (1937), with co-star Irene Dunne.

one-time fellow reporter. When she becomes engaged to another man, Charlie, aware of her fondness for fire engines and police cars, arranges to have many noise-making official vehicles show up at her door as "wedding presents." He himself drives up in an ambulance and makes off with a stunned Rusty atop a wagon marked "Insane Asylum."

Grant's flair for screwball comedy had at last expressed itself. So did his distaste for the Paramount contract system. Grant informed Paramount that he did not plan to renew. "It takes a good deal of courage to overcome obstacles in this business. If you're willing to go on for years being the sappy juvenile or ingenue, you're out before you know it. Only when you rebel do things really come your way...Only Mae West and Marlene Dietrich were permitted to choose their parts at Paramount. I was fed up with what I was doing," he later said. "It didn't turn out too badly. Without a contract, I pushed my money up to $300,000 a picture in no time."

Grant's first hand-picked film was *Riches and Romance* (1936), a British Grand National picture shot in England and released there under the title *The Amazing Quest of Ernest Bliss*. Grant plays Ernest Bliss, a very rich, young man who suffers from underwork. In the story, Bliss wagers his physician fifty thousand pounds that he can earn his own living for at least a year without resorting to his wealth. A few days before he is scheduled to win his bet, Frances, his girlfriend, unaware of Bliss's wealth, says she must marry her boss in order to provide a home for her sick sister. Bliss confesses to being wealthy, winning the girl, of course, but losing the wager. This was the screen's second adaptation of E. Phillips Oppenheim's novel, the first having been a 1921 silent version.

Back in the United States, this time with Columbia, Grant filmed *When You're in Love* (1937) with Grace Moore. Grant plays Jimmy Hudson, a well-to-do artist living in the United States near the Mexican border. Miss Moore (who actually was an accomplished opera soprano) plays Louise Fuller, a Mexican vocalist who needs a quick marriage to a United States citizen so she can appear in the States at a music festival. Hudson fits the bill.

Publicity photograph, *The Awful Truth* (1937), with canine star Mr. Smith ("Asta" of the *Thin Man* series).

The Toast of New York (1937) represented Grant's first contractual agreement with RKO studios. The setting of the film is fashionable nineteenth–century Wall Street, and the plot involves a love triangle with Frances Farmer portraying the actress Josie Mansfield, mistress of tycoon Jim Fisk (Edward Arnold). Nick Boyd (Grant) completes the triangle. By the final reel, tycoon Fisk is slain, thereby freeing Josie and Nick to begin a life together.

Grant's next role was in a very special zany comedy, Thorne Smith's *Topper* (1937). Independent producer Hal Roach brought in Norman Z. McLeod to direct the film, having a superb cast in mind. McLeod arranged for Grant and Constance Bennett to play George and Marion Kerby, husband and wife who return from the dead after an auto crash to liven up the stuffy existence of Cosmo Topper (Roland Young), a henpecked, rather dull, but lovable bank president. The Kerbys appear and disappear at will and harrass Topper in an affectionate, pushy sort of way. Mr. Young's Topper was a characterization of a milquetoast developing confidence, and the performance earned him an Oscar nomination. The movie, one of 1937's most popular, has remained a favorite of film buffs over the years.

Returning from Europe on the S.S. *Normandie,* with fellow passenger Marlene Dietrich, 1938.

At a costume party with date Phyllis Brooks, 1937.

Grant, a hot property now, chose his next project wisely. *The Awful Truth* (1937), directed by Leo McCarey, was a hilarious comedy about a divorcing couple's relationship during the ninety-day interlocutory period. Irene Dunne and Ralph Bellamy co-star as the soon-to-be-divorced pair. The film won one Oscar (for Best Director) and was nominated for four others. *The Awful Truth* confirmed to the movie world that Grant's talent was no fluke, his charisma, no passing inspiration.

Grant then turned to RKO for a prime role that Ronald Colman, Robert Montgomery, and Ray Milland had turned down — the introverted, distinguished paleontologist David Huxley in *Bringing Up Baby* (1938). Susan Vance (Katharine Hepburn) is cast as a wealthy woman with pet leopard named "Baby." Huxley, completing work on the reconstruction of a huge dinosaur skeleton, meets Susan, and immediately she begins to disrupt the professor's work. George, her aunt's terrier, makes off with one of Huxley's precious bones and buries it; Baby escapes at the same time; the search for the bone begins. Bizarre scenes include singing the leopard to sleep, Huxley being discovered in a negligee, Susan ripping the back of her dress at dinner one night, and the huge dinosaur skeleton — the professor's life's work — crashing down. Charles Ruggles, May Robson, and Barry Fitzgerald also appear in this highly successful farce.

Said Grant of his co-star: "Working with Kate Hepburn was incredible. You never saw such timing. She had a mind like a computer — every detail worked out. Yet computers don't have instincts, and her instincts were infallible. She taught me just about everything I know about comedy" Hepburn, too, complimented Grant: "He's a delicious personality who has learned to do certain things marvelously well. He has a lovely sense of timing and an amusing face and lovely voice."

Grant's next film was again with Katharine Hepburn: *Holiday* (1938). Donald Ogden Stewart adapted Philip Barry's successful play of the same name for the screen; Hepburn bought her way out of a strangling RKO contract; and George Cukor arranged to direct. In the story, Linda Seton (Hepburn) is a New York City snob and nonconformist whose sister is engaged to Johnny Case (Grant). Johnny ventures to New York to meet his fiance's family and ends up falling in love with Linda. The Setons are stereotypes of wealthy conservatives, and Johnny's philosophy of vacationing while you're young only to gain employment in one's later years upsets the family, but not Linda — she identifies with Johnny's radicalism.

By 1939, Grant had made thirty-one films, had accumulated substantial savings, was a solid box-office bet, and was a bachelor in Hollywood. To an interviewer's question he answered: "Contented? Rather! Here I am earning

Grant and Katharine Hepburn on the set of *Bringing Up Baby* (1938).

a pleasant living in the one exciting place left on the globe. The gods are good."

Grant made three pictures in 1939: *Gunga Din, Only Angels Have Wings,* and *In Name Only.* All three were dramatic films, but somehow casting Grant in a movie now required that his parts afford him at least occasional wit and charm. In *Gunga Din,* for example, his role called for a strong physical presence with little dialogue, but some of the dramatic sequences are tinged with Grant-style humor. In one scene, for instance, he marches alone into a band of enemy cutthroats and announces: "You're all under arrest." In another, he tries to overpower a man twice his size. Both efforts, of course, were wryly ineffectual.

Columbia boss Harry Cohn had ordered that a script be prepared to feature Grant with Jean Arthur. The result was Howard Hawks's *Only Angels Have Wings* (1939). The story is set in a South American port of call and concerns a tightly-knit group of bachelor pilots who fly mail over the Andes. The aerial sequences and Hawks-like scenes of the camaraderie among men with a shared cause are most dramatically successful and true.

In Name Only (1939) features Grant as Alec Walker, a wealthy man married to a gold digger (Kay Francis). On vacation in Connecticut, he meets Julie Eden (Carole Lombard), a young widow. They begin an affair, and Alec requests a divorce from his wife. She refuses, and Alec overdoses on alcohol and contracts pneumonia. A confrontation takes place between Mrs. Walker and Julie Eden, and the audience is left with the hope that Alec and Julie will one day be united.

When France and Great Britain declared war on Germany in 1939, Grant flew to Washington to confer with the British Ambassador. The diplomat advised him to stay in Hollywood and encourage other Britons there to raise money for, and make films sympathetic to, the Allied cause.

Grant began the decade of the Forties by performing again in a Howard Hawks production for Columbia. This time it was in the comedy *His Girl Friday.* (The 1928 Ben Hecht-Charles MacArthur Broadway hit was better known as *The Front Page,* and had been filmed in 1931 by Lewis Milestone; however, this 1940 production would be a star-studded, expanded version of the original.) Rosalind Russell plays Hildy Johnson, a journalist who decides to give up her career for married life in Albany, New York, to dull, but dignified, Bruce Baldwin (Ralph Bellamy). Hildy's ex-husband, newspaperman Walter Burns (Grant), learns of her plans and tries to dissuade her from taking the leap.

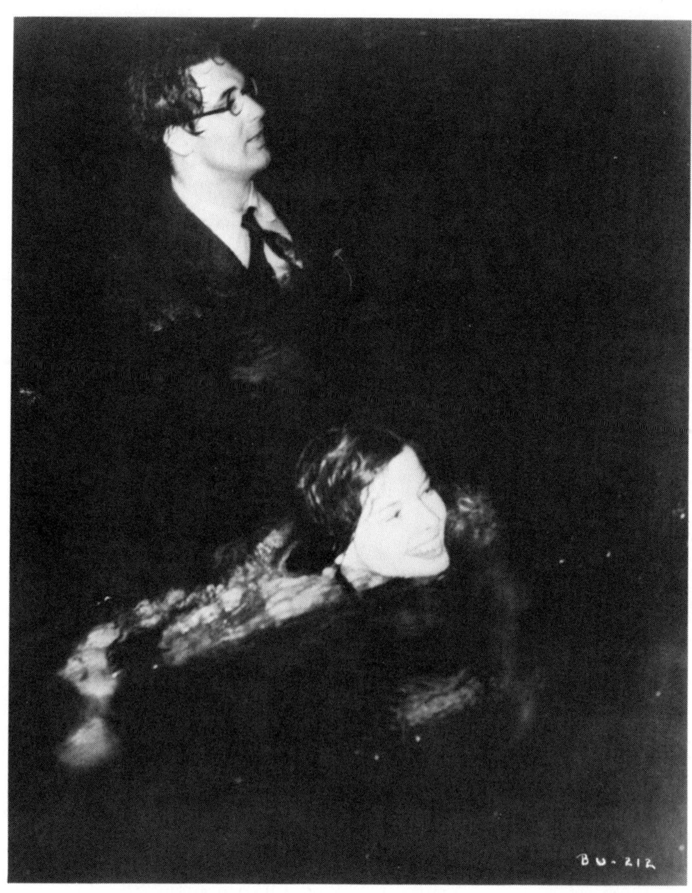

(Above & right) On the set of *Bringing Up Baby* (1938), with Katharine Hepburn.

Returning to RKO for his second film of 1940, *My Favorite Wife,* Grant was reunited with Irene Dunne. Director Leo McCarey, injured in an auto accident, was replaced by Garson Kanin. The prominent actor Granville Bates makes his last screen appearance in this

movie as a wisecracking judge. In the story, Grant plays a man who remarries—only to discover that his first wife, thought to be dead, has reappeared on the scene. (She had been marooned on a desert island for seven years with another man, Randolph Scott.) The character played by Scott poses enough of a challenge to Grant's character for audiences to wonder which man will win Miss Dunne.

Frank Lloyd's *The Howards of Virginia* (1940) was Grant's next vehicle. Based on the first section of Elizabeth Page's epic novel *The Tree of Liberty,* it is a Revolutionary War saga, a family narrative with much dialogue and little action. Parts of the movie were used for the 1941 compilation film *Land of Liberty.* Grant received mixed reviews.

Grant's final performance in 1940 was in the role of C.K. Dexter Haven in *The Philadelphia Story* (1940). Katharine Hepburn, who had starred in this Philip Barry play on Broadway, owned the screen rights and was cast as the female lead, Tracy Lord. George Cukor, Hepburn's favorite director, was assigned by MGM to the anticipated sure-fire hit; and James Stewart, Ruth Hussey, Roland Young, and John Howard were signed to co-star. Donald Ogden Stewart wrote the screen adaptation, for which he later won an Oscar.

The story begins with a reporter (James Stewart) and his photographer (Ruth Hussey) crashing the Philadelphia high-society celebration of the Lord family on the occasion of Tracy Lord's second marriage. C.K. Dexter Haven (Grant), Tracy's first husband, also shows up uninvited. The blue-blooded family is quite upset by the presence of these surprise guests. It becomes apparent that Tracy and Dexter had divorced primarily for reasons relating to Tracy's snobbishness. During the party, Miss Lord gradually begins to regret her elitist ways and develops compassion and other benevolent traits. While taking an innocent midnight dip in her pool with the reporter (Stewart), she is accidentally discovered by her fiance (John Howard) who is then prepared to cancel the wedding. Let the wedding go on, orders Tracy, but I'll remarry Dexter instead.

The Philadelphia Story was a smashing success. In a year of predominantly mindless Hollywood entertainment, this 1941 production infused some intelligence and sophisticated humor into the season's offerings.

On January 26, 1941, upon learning that his aunt and uncle and their daughter and son-in-law had been killed in an air raid on Bristol, Grant forwarded his more than $62,000 profit from *The Philadelphia Story* to the British war relief fund. He then traveled to England to make sure his mother was well and comfortable. (His father, had passed away in 1935 from an alcoholic liver failure.)

When Grant returned to California, friend Dorothy di Grasso introduced him to Woolworth heiress Barbara Hutton. It appeared that they had much in common and at first they got

Grant KO's actor Abner Biberman in *Gunga Din* (1939).

With Rita Hayworth (l.) and Jean Arthur in *Only Angels Have Wings* (1939).

along famously. Hutton had experienced her share of life's trials. She had been married twice and both times lost over a million dollars in settlements. Like Grant, she had grown up in a turbulent home. Her mother had jumped to her death from a hotel window when Barbara was five years old. Her father had been too busy to spend time with his daughter and left her in boarding schools and with distant relatives. For these, and other reasons, Grant and Hutton began to see quite a bit of each other.

In early 1941, as his romance with Barbara Hutton bloomed, Grant filmed *Penny Serenade*. A recording of the title song is played by Julie (Irene Dunne) in the film's opening scene as she readies to leave her husband Roger (Grant). Then, a series of flashbacks reveals their courtship: at its start, he is a newspaperman, she a saleswoman in a music store. An earthquake during their honeymoon causes the miscarriage of their unborn child, and Julie is no longer able to bear children. They adopt a child and raise her for six years until tragedy strikes again and takes her away. Grief all but finishes Julie and Roger's marriage, but the prospect of another adoption brings them together again. The melodramatic *Penny Serenade* succeeded with moviegoers and Grant

Filming, *Only Angels Have Wings* (1939). Grant (fourth from l.), director Howard Hawks, Noel Coward (c.), visiting the set, and (standing) actors Thomas Mitchell and Jean Arthur.

(Above) At home, 1940. Photograph by John Swope.

(Right) With Grant Horn, 1940. Photograph by John Swope.

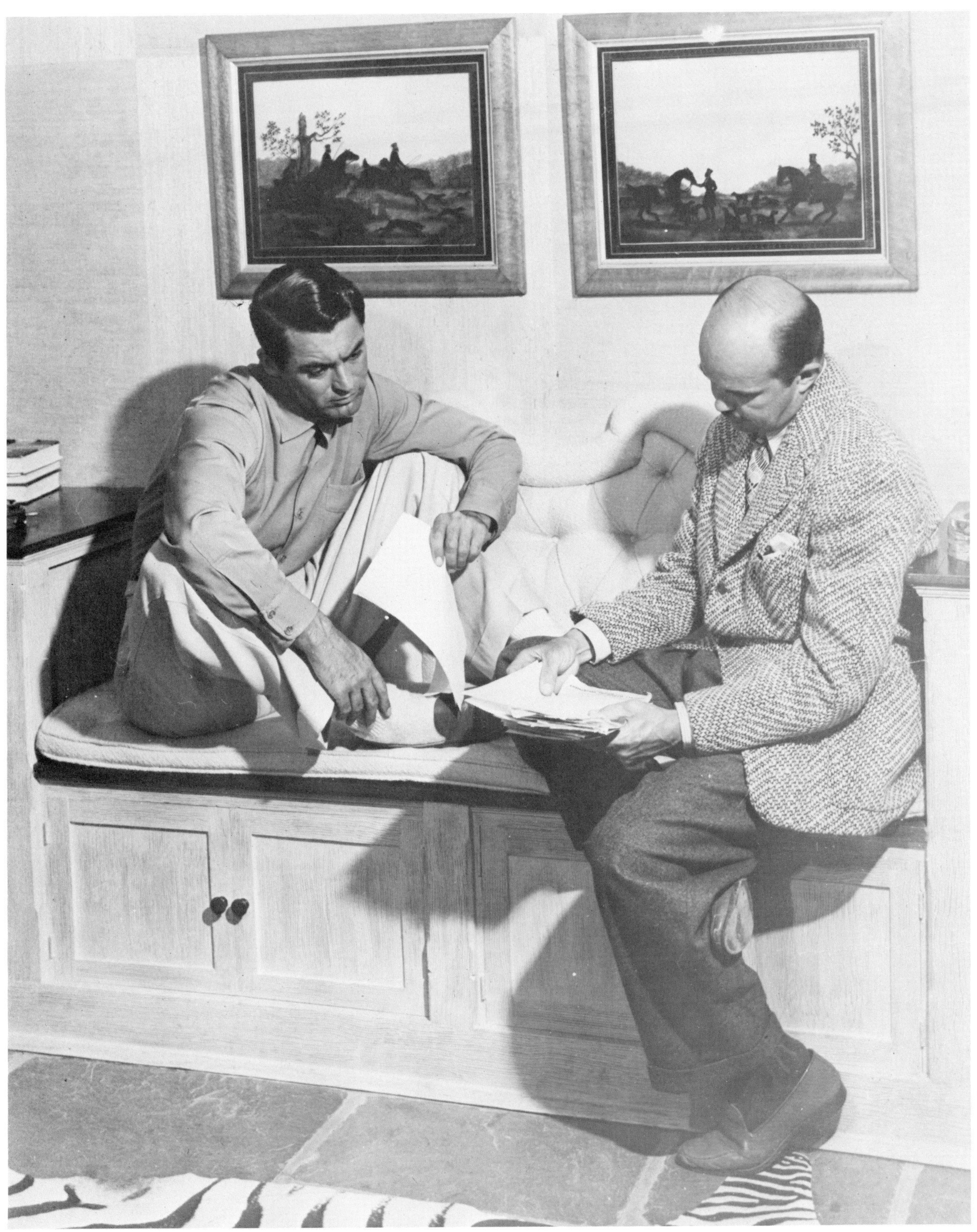

Publicity photograph, *His Girl Friday* (1940), with director Howard Hawks (c.) and co-star Rosalind Russell.

On location for *The Howards of Virginia* (1940), with Dickie Lyon.

received his first Oscar nomination. (Gary Cooper won the Oscar that year for his performance in *Sergeant York.)*

Grant spent the summer of 1941 vacationing in Mexico with some friends, Barbara Hutton among them. He relished the privacy allowed them.

Suspicion, Grant's first film with director Alfred Hitchcock, was released in November of 1941. It is about Johnny Aysgarth— a charming young Briton, but a thief and a liar since his school days—who sincerely falls in love and marries heiress Lina McLaidlaw (Joan Fontaine). Johnny becomes involved in an embezzling scheme, and a close friend of his dies under mysterious circumstances. Johnny's wife suspects him of murdering the friend and fears she will be his next victim. Finally, she confronts him and discovers that he has no intention of killing her.

Suspicion was based on the popular Francis Iles novel *Before the Fact,* which contains a radically different ending (Johnny *is* a killer and *does* murder his wife), but the RKO producers found that ending unacceptable for presentation to the film-viewing public. Hitchcock, at that point in his career, was unable to prevent critical script changes and, along with Grant, was disturbed by this kind of managerial interference. *Suspicion* is the only Grant–Hitchcock film to have been tampered with by management and the only one not to gross at least $4 million at the box office.

In late 1941, director Frank Capra brought several members of the Broadway cast of *Arsenic and Old Lace* to the West Coast to make a screen version of the hit play. When Bob Hope turned down the role of Mortimer, Grant accepted it. *Arsenic and Old Lace* is a wild tale about two Brooklyn Heights spinsters who "mercifully" poison their lonely, elderly visitors. Mortimer Brewster (Grant) visits his crazy aunts (Josephine Hull and Jean Adair) with his new bride Elaine (Priscilla Lane). Unfortunately for Mortimer, he discovers a body in a windowseat and becomes the next target of another mad relative's vengeance. The police arrive in time to save the young couple, and Mr. Witherspoon (Edward Everett Horton), the superintendant of "Happydale Sanitarium," accompanies the old ladies to where they will cause no further harm. Before they leave, though, the aunts tell Mortimer that he was adopted and is therefore not blood-related to the Brewster family. Relieved at not having a genetic madness to look forward to, Mortimer embraces Elaine.

Horsing around with actress Martha Scott on the set of *The Howards of Virginia* (1940).

Because of the ensuing world war and a

With Katharine Hepburn in *The Philadelphia Story* (1940).

With Joan Fontaine in a scene from *Suspicion* (1941).

3

Grant receives U.S. citizenship papers in federal court, L.A., 1942.

particular contractual clause preventing the release of the film until the play had closed in New York, *Arsenic and Old Lace* was not shown in movie theaters until 1944. In fact, American troops in North Africa were the first to view it at a battlefield premiere in 1943.

Early in 1942, Grant traveled with a group of stars making a three-week whistle-stop tour of the United States. He often spoke and performed on his own during the tour and also appeared as straight man to Bert Lahr. The train would arrive in each town in the morning, the afternoon was passed with local receptions, and the celebrities would perform in the evening.

In June of 1942, Grant became an American citizen and had his name legally changed from Archibald Leach to Cary Grant. In July, 1942, he and Barbara Hutton were married in a six-minute ceremony in the home of Grant's business manager. It was discovered later that Grant had signed a paper relinquishing any claim to Miss Hutton's fortune should they ever divorce.

The newlyweds moved into a beach house near where Grant and Scott had lived before. The standard of living, however, was not sufficient for Hutton, so she rented Douglas Fairbanks, Jr.'s mansion for them in Pacific Palisades. With them lived eleven servants, Hutton's son, Lance (by a previous husband), Lance's nurse, Hutton's secretary, and Grant's valet. Grant remembers that Hutton ordered daily papers for everyone in the house, which very much annoyed him. "I'd come home from the studio at night, park my car in the garage, and on the patio I'd wade through eleven copies of the *Evening Herald and Express.* I'd say to Barbara: 'Now, why does each servant have to have his own special copy of the paper?' [She replied] she thought they wouldn't like sharing." It was an honest, natural response and, perhaps, symptomatic of Hutton's true aristocracy—something Grant could not recognize because he was only superficially aristocratic. He had acquired, through study,taste, style, and savoir-faire; but at heart he was still, as Randolph Scott concluded, "a regular guy."

Grant stayed busy. Working with director George Stevens for Columbia and again with

Some horseplay during a party thrown by the Marx brothers, 1942; Groucho (c.) and Desi Arnez (r.).

(Left) On a tour of settlement houses in New York's lower East Side, 1943, Grant stops to lift a little girl at the Hamilton House on Market Street. At left is Don Barclay, noted vaudevillian with whom Grant appeared as a "stooge" many years ago.

Jean Arthur, he filmed *The Talk of the Town* (1942). In the story, Leopold Dilg (Grant) is being hunted on a phony murder and arson charge. Nora Shelley (Jean Arthur) agrees to hide him in the house she has just rented to Michael Lightcap (Ronald Colman), a law school dean who plans to spend a quiet summer writing. Of course, it doesn't work out the way he expected.

The opportunity to make a film with Ginger Rogers greatly appealed to Grant, so he agreed to star in *Once Upon a Honeymoon* (1942), a Leo McCarey–RKO picture. Grant plays Pat O'Toole, a radio correspondent assigned to Europe in 1938. There he meets Kate (Ginger Rogers), a former American burlesque queen married to Baron Von Luber (Walter Slezak), a secret Nazi agent. Pat trails Von Luber, hoping to uncover evidence of his espionage. In the process of exposing the Baron, Pat falls in love with Kate, whom he eventually marries when the Baron's activities are made public.

Grant next starred in *Mr. Lucky* (1943), a new kind of film for him. Previously he had always had either a superlative supporting cast, a great story, or some other source of support to help make any project of his a success.

(Above) Exclusive photograph of Grant with Barbara Hutton, his second wife, paid for by Louella Parsons, 1943.

(Right) At home, having an ice cream soda, 1944.

The weight of *Mr. Lucky,* however, rested solely on Grant's shoulders; it had little else going for it. In the story, Grant plays Joe, a gambler and owner of a gambling ship. He and his associates are seeking money to bankroll operations in the South Atlantic when three of them are nailed by the draft board. Joe assumes the identity of a dead friend to escape the draft and pursue his "profession." He weasels his way into a war relief operation and persuades them to let him run a gambling concession at their fund-raising ball. During this time, he finds out that the identity he assumed was of an ex-convict who needed only one more conviction to be sentenced to a life term. He falls in love with an heiress who eventually re-educates him to lead a life of honesty.

As World War II headed into its decisive

With Ted Donaldson and Janet Blair in *Once Upon A Time* (1944).

stages in 1944, Grant wanted very much to be in the war movie *Destination Tokyo* (1944) and arranged with Warner Bros. to do so. He had director approval, and when he learned that screenwriter Delmer Daves was being considered to direct his first picture, Grant expressed confidence in him. "I asked Cary," said Daves later, "what had inspired his approval. He told me that once upon a time Mae West had pointed to him and said, 'I approve that young man. I think he'll be my new leading man,' and as a result, a career was born. Cary,

With Priscilla Lane in *Arsenic and Old Lace* (1944).

knowing me as a friend and having seen and liked many of the pictures I had written, felt that I would make a good director and so why not be the first man to say, 'I have faith in Delmer Daves.' "

Destination Tokyo concerns the crew of the *Copperfin,* a United States submarine. On Christmas eve, 1942, Captain Cassidy (Grant) receives his orders to proceed to Japan. On the way, the sub rendezvous with an American plane to pick up a meteorologist who, with crewmen Wolf (John Garfield) and Sparks

On location for *Notorius* (1946), with co-star Ingrid Bergman and director Alfred Hitchcock.

Attending a party at Romanoff's, 1946, with director Alfred Hitchcock (behind Grant's head) and Mrs. Paul Henreid.

(John Forsythe) will go ashore at Tokyo to gain information vital to the United States Navy for its planned attack on the Japanese capital city. The three men succeed in their mission, and before the *Copperfin* flees the harbor, it torpedos and sinks a Japanese carrier. "Even moviegoers who have developed a severe allergy for service pictures should find *Destination Tokyo* the high among the superior films of the war," said *Newsweek*.

After *Destination Tokyo,* Grant sought lighter material for a change of pace. That he found in *Once Upon a Time* (1944) in which he plays Jerry Flynn, a theatrical producer who is about to have his theater closed. In the story, Flynn tosses a nickel over his shoulder. It is picked up by a boy named Pinky (Ted Donaldson) who carries inside a shoe box the dancing

Grant and Ingrid Bergman in *Notorious* (1946).

"Curly the Wonder Worm." Through the efforts of Flynn, the toe-tapping caterpillar becomes a sensation. However, the film did not.

The last film Grant made in 1944 was *None but the Lonely Heart.* Clifford Odets, who wrote the screen adaptation of Richard Llewellyn's novel was asked to direct the film. Later he explained how he came to do so: "When I met Cary Grant for the first time, he said to me, 'I'd like you to direct me in this picture.' I explained that I had never directed anyone, let alone Cary Grant, but he told me if I

was only seven years old when my mother and Cary were married, but I remember that he was a marvelous father to me. He was so warm and charming and I loved going to the studio with him. He was very good with children."

None but the Lonely Heart is a poignant story about a young Englishman, Ernie Mott (Grant) and his mother (Ethel Barrymore). Mott joins a band of thieves in an effort to relieve his mother's poverty, and she opens up a secondhand store and becomes a "fence" to accumulate money to leave to her son. (She is dying of cancer.) Grant's strong performance earned him another Academy Award nomination, but he did not win that year either.

On August 15, 1944, Grant separated from his wife, Barbara Hutton. "There is no thought of divorce at the present time," said Hutton. "Cary and I are remaining the fondest of friends." They continued to live in the same house, however, partly because of a wartime housing shortage, and partly because Hutton's former husband had abducted their son Lance and had fled to Canada. During the trying battle for custody of her son, Grant felt he ought to remain with her. "Cary decided to stand by me," Hutton said later to reporters, "but I think it's best that we part now. Besides, it's dishonest and unfair to take advantage of his name and protection because I am fighting to hold my child."

In August, 1945, a year after their separation, Barbara Hutton marched into court and addressed the judge: "Cary didn't like my friends and I didn't like his friends. When I had my friends to dinner, he would stay in bed. On the few occasions that he joined us, he just didn't seem amused. He was too bored and it was all very embarrassing to me."

Said Cary: "My hope was to get affection. I didn't know I had to give it, too. Our interests were not the same. I was more interested in my work than I should have been, I suppose. I still have a great feeling for her. We are great and good friends." Their divorce was granted.

Lance, Hutton's son, always spoke of Grant as his favorite stepfather. (Hutton was to marry several times after her divorce from Grant.) "I could write the words, I should certainly be able to direct their use. So maybe Cary doesn't own a string of race horses, but if he believes in you, he's willing to gamble his whole career on you."

The only film Grant made in 1945 was *Night and Day* (released in 1946), a story based on the life of Cole Porter. It is Grant's first appearance in Technicolor. The Cole Porter story according to the somewhat fictitious *Night and Day,* ran as follows: at Yale in 1914, young Porter writes songs for school productions; war breaks out; Porter joins the forces in Europe and receives a leg wound. Returning home, he struggles as an aspiring songwriter, suffers the belittlement that his family heaps upon him, but eventually achieves success. Grant sings "An Old Fashioned Garden," "Miss Otis Regrets," and "You're the Top"—all rendered with style.

Michael Curtiz directed the musical in a manner that did not please Grant. Grant wrote to him later: "Mike, now that the last foot of the film is shot, I want you to know that if I'm ever stupid enough to be caught working with you, you'll know I'm either broke or I've lost my mind. You may bamboozle crews and cameramen to work with you, but not me, not again."

In 1946, Grant made a guest appearance in John Wayne's *Without Reservations.* He appeared in only one other film that year—Alfred Hitchcock's *Notorious.* In this film, Ingrid Bergman plays Alicia Huberman, a German-American whose father has been convicted of treason. She meets Devlin (Grant), an American intelligence officer assigned to assess her patriotism. Devlin concludes that Alicia would be perfect for espionage work in Rio de Janeiro where I.G. Farben, a German chemical cartel, is up to no good. Upon arriving in Brazil, Alicia meets Alexander Sebastian (Claude Rains), Farben's number one man, who becomes infatuated with her, and soon asks her to marry him. She reluctantly does so, considering it part of her job. (She and Devlin are in love.) Through a series of incidents involving wine bottles and keys, she discovers that uranium is being

Grant swaps confidences with date Betty Hensel at a Hollywood cocktail party, 1946. Danny Kaye, sucking on the pit of his cocktail olive, observes.

stored in bottles in her husband's wine cellar. Alexander soon realizes that his wife has betrayed him; he also knows that he is being watched by his co-conspirators and cannot let on that he has compromised the Nazi cause for love. He consults his mother (Madame Konstantin) who advises him that slow poisoning of Alicia is his only way out. When Alicia misses a rendezvous with Devlin, he goes to the Sebastian home, finds her nearly unconscious, and escorts her out of the house as Alexander begs them to stay.

Notorious received two Oscar nominations: one earned by Rains and one by Ben Hecht, the screenwriter. Regarded now as one of Hitchcock's minor masterpieces, *Notorious* was received without enthusiasm by the critics in the mid-forties. The *Canadian Forum:* "Not that *Notorious* is precisely a dull picture, but we have seen so many of its kind lately... Either because the *Casablanca* cycle of movies has left us blase, glutted with the type, or because Hitchcock himself has slipped into a rut, *Notorious* seems to lack pace..."

At the Macambo Club, 1947, with date Betty Hensel.

Grant made two pictures in 1947: a comedy, *The Bachelor and the Bobby Soxer,* and *The Bishop's Wife*. In *The Bachelor...,* Dick (Grant) appears before a judge (Myrna Loy) in an assault case stemming from a street scuffle. The charges are dismissed for lack of evidence. Dick, an artist, is scheduled to lecture the following day at a local high school. The judge's kid sister Susan (Shirley Temple) attends the lecture and falls in love with him. Dick, then, pretends to be Susan's boyfriend until her infatuation wears off. The comedy reaches its peak with Grant's mimicking of Temple's adolescent slang, which does not amuse the judge.

The Bishop's Wife was RKO's 1947 contribution to the Christmas season. Grant plays Dudley, an angel who comes to the aid of Henry Brougham (David Niven). Brougham is an Episcopalian bishop who prays for funds to help build a new cathedral, but his prayers go unanswered. Dudley sees that Henry is losing faith and that his marriage is troubled, so he sets about to make Henry's wife (Loretta Young) more romantic, happy, and responsive. In the end, the new church remains unbuilt, but the bishop's small house is happier and more hopeful than it was before the angel's arrival.

Miss Young noted Grant's perfectionist at-

Tying Loretta Young's skate during a lull in production of *The Bishop's Wife* (1947).

(Left) On the set of *The Bishop's Wife* (1947), with co-stars Loretta Young and David Niven (r.).

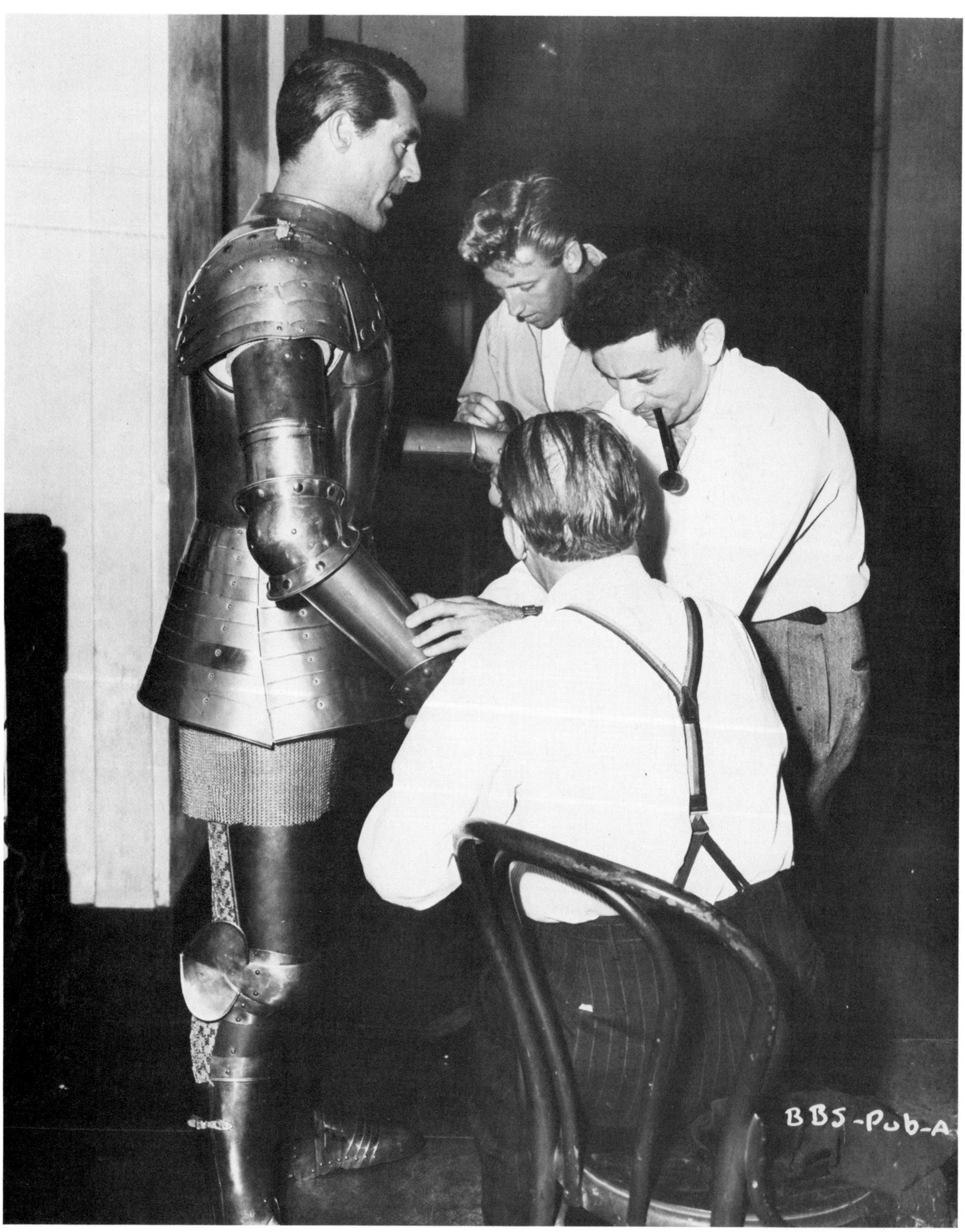
BBS-Pub-A

Shirley Temple knits, Johnny Sands (r.) downs ice cream, Grant looks on between scenes of *The Bachelor And The Bobby-Soxer* (1947).

(Left) Grant being suited in armor for a scene in *The Bachelor And The Bobby-Soxer* (1947). Assisting the wardrobe men is director Irving Reis (with pipe).

titude with a touch of wonder and irritation: "There was one scene in which Cary and I were to enter a house. It was a snow scene, and as we started to stamp the snow from our boots before entering, Cary suddenly stopped short. 'Just a minute,' he said. 'If it's cold outside and the house is nice and warm inside, why isn't there any frost on the windows?' Production came to a complete halt while frustrated set dressers scurried about putting fake frost in the windows. Then and only then did we complete the scene."

Throughout the mid-Forties and especially in 1947, Grant chummed around with Howard Hughes. "Everytime I'm a bachelor again, Hughes calls up and suggests that we go and see what the world is made of." Together they made flying expeditions and planned a collaboration on a film series. "The movies would be set ten or so years in the future," Grant said in 1947. "The hero would belong to the world police. The plot would concern his adventures as he flies from one country to another battling intrigues against the peace of the world. A different picture would be made about each country, weaving its customs into the story." Grant and Hughes had outlined the James Bond success formula more than ten years before it would become someone's reality.

Early in 1948, Grant made *Mr. Blandings Builds His Dream House* with Myrna Loy and Melvyn Douglas. The story tells of a city couple who search for a home in rural Connecticut, but the realtor they contact sells them a lemon

Cary Gran

Grant and co-star Myrna Loy on the set of *Mr. Blandings Builds His Dream House* (1948).

With Myrna Loy between scenes of *Mr. Blandings Builds His Dream House* (1948).

and the trouble begins. In the end, they tear down the old house and build their "dream house."

In the summer of 1948, Grant traveled to England, and on the voyage home aboard the *Queen Mary,* he was introduced by actress Merle Oberon to Betsy Drake, a young actress who had recently finished a successful run in London in the play *Deep Are the Roots.* Betsy had grown up in the Washington, D.C. area and had gone to high school in Virginia. Her grandfather, a wealthy Chicago architect, had lost a fortune in the 1929 stock market crash. Miss Drake had studied theater for two years in college before embarking on her professional career. "I told Merle to go tell Betsy she had to lunch with a lonely man. Except for that night, when she had a previous date, I snagged her for

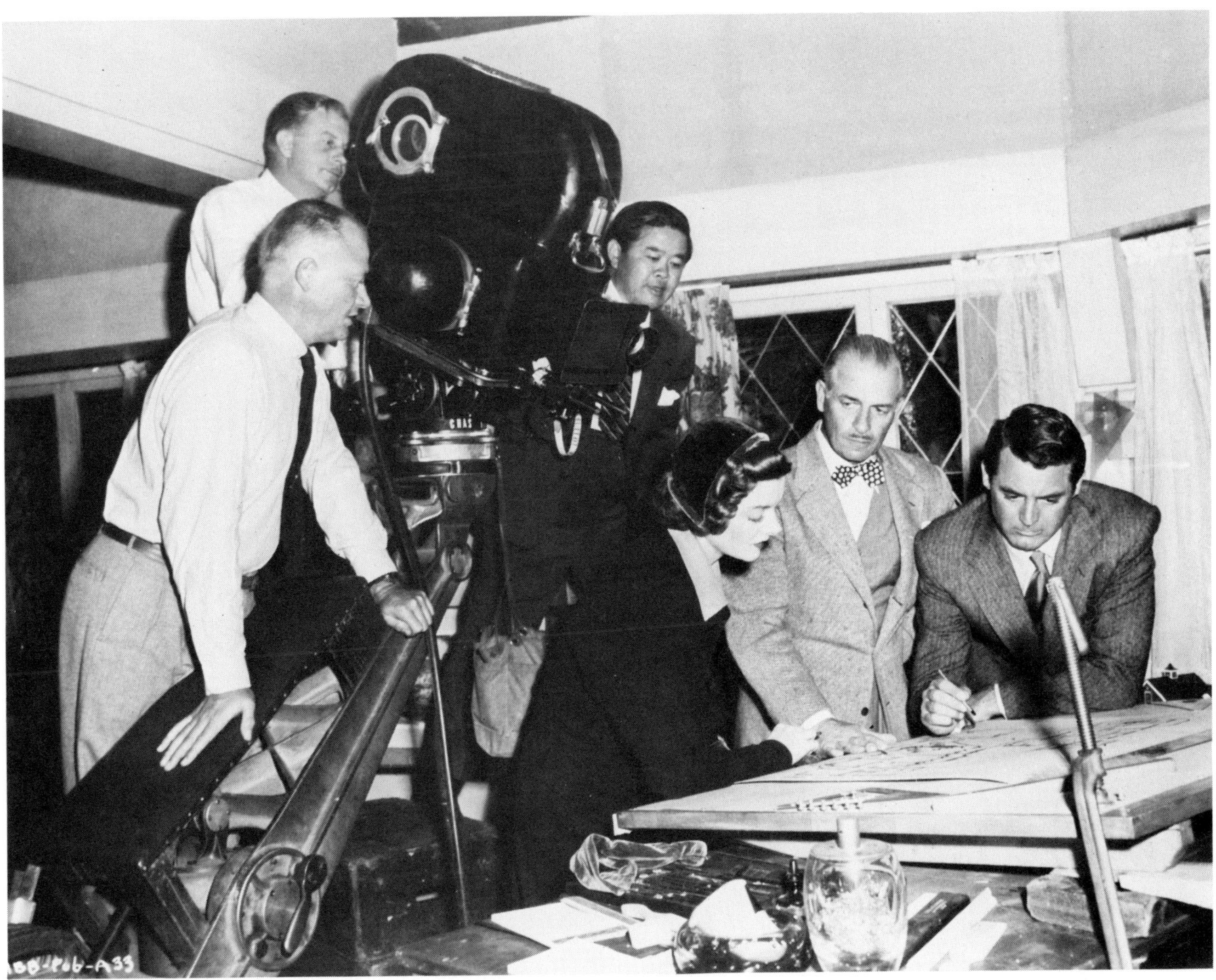

On the set of *Mr. Blandings Builds His Dream House* (1948). Left to right: director H.C. Potter, cinematographer James Wong Howe, Myrna Loy, Reginald Denny, and Grant.

every meal of the crossing."

Back in Hollywood, Grant introduced Miss Drake to producers David O. Selznick and Dore Schary, among others. She was then cast as the leading lady opposite Grant in his next film, *Every Girl Should Be Married* (1948), a familiar girl-schemes-to-get-boy yarn. Drake had never before appeared on film, but her premiere performance was well received. She was, however,criticized for resorting to false mannerisms when acting inspiration failed her, but she was applauded for being a competent actress. *Every Girl Should Be Married* was Grant's final association with RKO but not with Drake. Very much impressed by her charm and intelligence, he began to date her frequently, and rumors that their·relationship had turned serious quickly spread.

On location in Heidelburg, Germany, for *I Was A Male War Bride* (1949).

With Ann Sheridan during filming of *I Was A Male War Bride* (1949).

Grant and actress Betsy Drake phone Hollywood friends after their marriage, Dec. 25, 1949.

In 1949, Ann Sheridan and Cary Grant made a splendid comedy team in Howard Hawks *I Was A Male War Bride*. French Captain Henri Rochard (Grant) has an assistant in Europe, Lieutenant Catherine Gates (Sheridan), a WAC officer. At first they squabble, but eventually they fall in love and marry. The comedy lies in their efforts to get Captain Rochard into the United States, where they plan to live. It seems immigration regulations will accept Rochard only as a "war bride." Their problem is to meet immigration requirements without

Met by wife Betsy Drake after returning from filming *I Was A Male War Bride* (1949) in Europe. Grant sailed home on a slow freighter to recuperate from hepatitis.

breaking any army regulations. It's all a farce, of course. The new comedy team of Grant and Sheridan appeared to have a bright future, but no vehicle comparable to *I Was A Male War Bride* came their way again.

Miss Sheridan commented on the routine of filming *I Was A Male War Bride:* "Howard Hawks would sit on the set and he'd say, 'Well, I'm not quite satisfied with this scene. What would you say in a situation like this? So we'd sit and think, and it was inevitably Cary [who] would tell you what to say. Howard is a very clever man. He picked brains. And he had a very clever brain to pick [in] Cary Grant, believe me. If only Cary had directed. I begged him. I said, 'Please get something and direct it before I'm too old to play comedy,' and he said, 'No, no dear, too much work.' "

During the filming of *I Was A Male War Bride,* Grant came down with jaundice. While he was recovering, Betsy Drake was almost constantly at his side. On Christmas day, 1949, they were married in Phoenix, Arizona, with Howard Hughes acting as Grant's best man. Unfortunately, there was no time to honeymoon because of Grant's film commitments. They immediately moved into a six-room Beverly Hills ranch house. Betsy stayed home, developing her hobbies. (She had a telescope and she loved books. In fact, she'd buy twenty to thirty volumes at a time. This annoyed Grant because he found himself constantly removing stacks of books from chairs and sofas.) They lived a very domestic life in contrast to the Hutton style. "We get up in the morning," said Drake, "put on blue jeans or shorts, sit around drinking coffee, and discuss everything from God to the garment industry...He always wakes up in fine humor." They rarely went to posh nightclubs or restaurants, nor did they entertain very often; they lived a simple, relatively unglamorous life. Grant even took up horseback riding and became very skilled at it.

In *Crisis* (1950), Grant plays Dr. Eugene Ferguson, a renowned brain surgeon vacationing in a Latin American country. He is kidnapped, brought to the presidential palace, and made to operate on the ailing dictator (Jose Ferrer). The director of *Crisis,* Richard Brooks, one of Grant's closest friends, tells this story about his relationship with Grant: "I don't know all the emotions which keep Cary from being frivolous with his money. I certainly wouldn't call him penurious. I remember one Christmas when he and I exchanged expensive presents. We were both disturbed over that because I believe we both felt that this sort of thing is a favor-seeking device. We agreed not to exchange gifts again. Two years went by. Then I received in the mail a package wrapped in old newspapers from Hong Kong. It was a paperweight made from an old opium pipe. The card was from Cary and said he thought I would like this because I collect pipes. Later, an insurance company told me that the paperweight was solid silver and worth at least a thousand dollars. While he can give gifts, Cary finds it difficult to accept things from anyone—presents, compliments, or even love. He has a compulsion to feel free. Even when it comes to something as simple as having dinner with me, he will never say, 'How about dinner a week from Tuesday?' That's a commitment. If I'm free some night and Cary happens to be free that same night, then we'll have dinner together."

In 1951, Grant appeared in *People Will Talk,* a Joseph L. Mankiewicz film. He plays Dr. Noah Praetorious, a resident at a local hospital who treats an attempted suicide victim (Jeanne Crain) and learns of her despair over becoming the mother of an illegitimate child. Praetorious marries her, but she fears he has done so out of pity. The Mankiewicz script and direction infused the film with real-life drama, and critics hailed the picture. *Newsweek* called it a "sensi-

In the studio of sculptor Dezso Lanyi, 1950. Grant had asked the recently stricken sculptor to do a head of him.

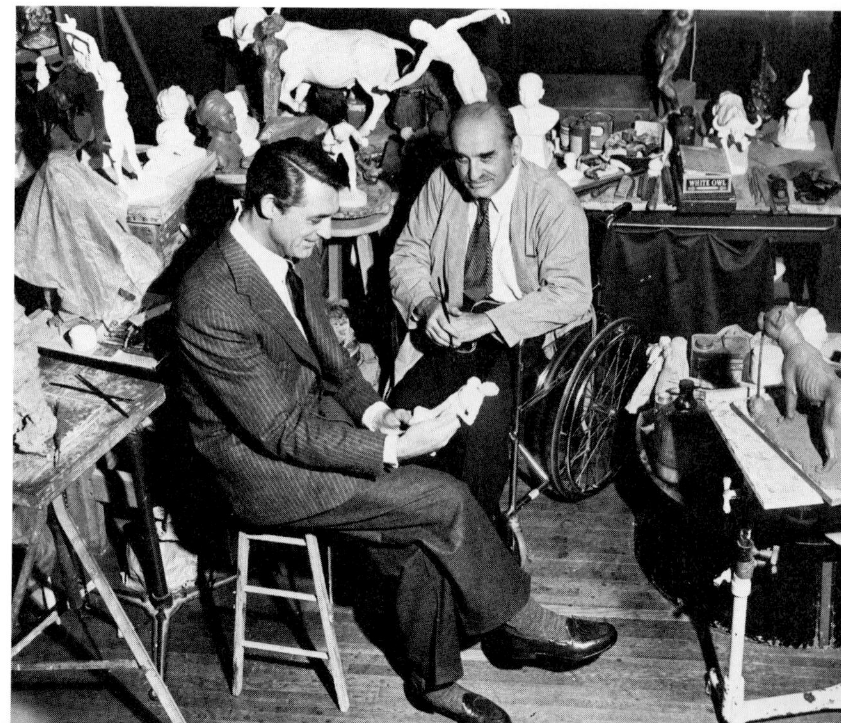

Giving advice to long-time friend Spencer Tracy before Tracy sailed on the *Queen Elizabeth* for Europe.

tive, impressive, very adult" film.

Grant next starred with wife Betsy Drake in *Room for One More* (1952). They play a married couple, the Roses, who have a small house and three children. Mrs. Rose has an exceedingly generous nature and accepts into their home all animals and humans requesting shelter. Thus, thirteen-year-old Jane, an unwanted child of divorced parents, comes for a short visit and ends up being adopted. A lad with leg braces makes his way into the Rose family as well. The film was popular in the United States, but European critics were much concerned with the film's depiction of American children. Continental observers detected indulgence and coddling, which did not sit well with them.

Again Grant reunited with director Howard Hawks and Twentieth Century-Fox to make *Monkey Business* (1952), a farce concerning a rejuvenating chemical. Grant, as Dr. Barnaby Fulton, discovers the formula for a drug that will regenerate damaged skin tissue and make healthy skin tissue look younger. A series of

With co-star Grace Kelly on location on the French Riviera during filming of *To Catch A Thief* (1955).

(Left) Dropping into character on his way to Europe, 1954, to play the part of a shady individual in *To Catch A Thief* (1955).

mix-ups ensue when Mrs. Fulton (Ginger Rogers) suspects Barnaby of falling for a company secretary (Marilyn Monroe) and of overdosing on his new drug discovery. Grant does, in fact, sip from his fountain of youth, and the scenes in which he regresses into a 1950s teenager are uproarious. *Monkey Business* was Grant's fifth and final picture with director Hawks.

Grant may have always seemed calm and in control on screen, but it was common knowledge around the set that he was "fit to be tied"

while filming. He sometimes changed his perspiration-soaked shirt three times in one scene. Some of his nervousness manifested itself in his reluctance to accept roles immediately upon their offering. For example, Grant had first crack at Gregory Peck's role in *Roman Holiday* and at Humphrey Bogart's role in *Sabrina*. He could even have starred with Judy Garland in *A Star Is Born,* but second thoughts and severe self-doubts haunted him.

Grant did, however, select *Dream Wife,* his sole endeavor of 1953. It was very much a "women's liberation" piece: bachelor Clemson Reade (Grant) wants his fiancee (Deborah Kerr) to mind the house after marriage; but she has independent notions. Reade recalls meeting Princess Tarji of Bukistan on a recent trip overseas and, because she has been raised to please men, proposes marriage to her via cable. When the Princess comes to the States, she meets Deborah Kerr, develops a taste for emancipation, and no longer wishes to fulfill the role of a "dream wife."

Later in 1953, Grant decided to retire from filmmaking. He was not exhausted as an actor as much as disgusted by the precarious future of comedy. "It was the period of blue jeans, the dope addicts, the Method, and nobody cared about comedy at all," he said. During this period, he had a chance to take a good look at himself and his marriage. He and Betsy Drake loved each other very much, but Grant was not a very tolerant man. He found it impossible to remain quiet when Betsy exhibited some harmless peccadillo. He was a critical perfectionist—not an ideal spouse for cooperative living. Still, both people were intelligent and sensitive, and they soon began exploring their inner selves through auto-hypnosis.

Grant once said: "Hypnotism is really utter, complete relaxation, which is the secret of success in everything from golf to acting to

On location for *To Catch A Thief* (1955). Grant and Grace Kelly listen to director Alfred Hitchcock.

Filming *To Catch A Thief* (1955). Grant and Grace Kelly are at right. Directly under the light is director Alfred Hitchcock.

(Right) Perched precariously on the rail of the S.S. *Mauretania,* flanked (l.) by wife Betsy Drake and (r.) actress Grace Kelly. The trio were returning from Europe, where Grant and Miss Kelly filmed *To Catch A Thief* (1955).

lovemaking." He even developed the ability to control his own nerve endings. "Since I can turn off pain in any part of my body, it isn't difficult to cut off feeling in one whole side of my face. My dentist and I have a signal. When I snap the fingers of my right hand, he starts drilling." A new world had opened up to Grant, an inner world. His explorations, which were to bloom fully in the 1960s, were blossoming in the 1950s. He later said: "I'm interested in any kind of self-improvement. Mankind has to be interested in self-improvement. If not, we might as well give up. You go from one plateau to another. If a man every five years faithfully puts down his views of life, love, and the world, at the end of twenty years he would find a frightful mass of

inconsistencies. People cannot stay the same. They change every second."

In the almost two years of professional idleness Grant had imposed on himself in 1953 and 1954, he hadn't lost interest in film entirely. He simply wished to wait for a compelling script to cross his desk. During this period, he referred to himself as "a quivering mass of indecision," and his loss of William Holden's role in *Bridge on the River Kwai* was one unfortunate consequence. "Columbia, knowing me, had also sent a script to Bill Holden. He read the story, decided it was magnificent, and said he'd do it. By then, of course, I realized what a great part I had lost."

It took director Alfred Hitchcock to convince Grant to make a new film. Hitchcock's *To Catch A Thief* (1955) was a popular success. Grace Kelly co-stars. Grant plays John Robie, a reformed jewel thief who comes under suspicion of the French gendarmes when a series of thefts occur in Cannes (where Robie resides). Each robbery bears his trademark: a well-planned, meticulously carried out heist with a clean getaway. Innocent of the crimes and desiring to clear his name, he sets out to catch the actual thief in the act.

After completing *To Catch A Thief,* Grant again went into semi-retirement, but then selected *The Pride and the Passion* (1957) as a return vehicle. This epic, directed by Stanley Kramer, deals with the Napoleonic Wars, from the Spanish point of view. Grant is a British naval officer who lands in Spain to prevent a huge cannon from falling into the hands of the occupying French. The cannon is the world's largest and a symbol of national unity to Spain. Frank Sinatra plays Miguel, a guerrilla leader who convinces Grant to use the cannon to drive the French from Avila, a town that functions as the center of the French occupation forces. With the cannon's help, Grant and Sinatra join forces to return Avila to Spain — despite their romantic rivalry over Juana, the obligatory spirited wartime wench, played by Sophia Loren.

The Pride and the Passion grossed only $4.5 million at the box office, nowhere near Grant's most successful effort. During the filming, Grant reportedly became enamoured of Sophia Loren ("Who wouldn't fall in love with her? She's a marvelous flirt," Grant said), and rumors about them began to spread. As a result, Betsy Drake flew to Spain to be with Grant for a short time. While returning home on the steamship *Andrea Doria* in July of 1956, she experienced firsthand a disaster that shocked the world. The *Doria* struck the vessel *Stockholm* off Nantucket Island and sank; fifty-one people died. Drake survived, and the moment the filming of *The Pride and the Passion* was completed, Grant returned home to be at his wife's side. So ended rumors about an affair with Loren.

In 1957, some eighteen years after director Leo McCarey had filmed *Love Affair* with Charles Boyer and Irene Dunne, McCarey decided to remake it under the title *An Affair To Remember* (1957). Grant and Deborah Kerr play the romantic leads. As the story unfolds, Nickie Ferrante (Grant) is on a transatlantic liner en route to New York to meet his fiancee. Terry McKay (Kerr) is doing likewise. They enjoy each other's company, but go separate ways once stateside. Six months later, Nickie tries to contact Terry; he eventually finds her; and they travel abroad to live happily ever after.

Grant's next film, *Kiss Them for Me* (1957), is a lightweight comedy with Suzy Parker, Jayne Mansfield, Ray Walston, and Larry Blyden. It tells the story of three World War II Navy fliers who go to San Francisco for a brief but raucous furlough. Partying with women in their hotel suite, they make a nuisance of themselves.

Next, Grant chose to film *Indiscreet* in 1958. He co-stars with Ingrid Bergman, an actress with whom Grant has shared a close friendship, a friendship that still thrives today. The story centers around a romance between the two principals: Grant is Phillip Adams, a lecturer on economics; Anna (Bergman) is an accomplished actress. They meet in London, and when Anna expresses a serious interest in Phillip, he warns her that he is married, but separated, and unable to get a divorce. Never-

With Mae West at a Hollywood night club, 1955. Grant turned out to wish his former leading lady well at the opening of her act.

With Sophia Loren during filming of *The Pride and the Passion* (1957).

theless, Anna desires him. Phillip departs for the United States, promising to return. During his absence, Anna discovers that Phillip is not married at all and never has been. He is a bachelor with "a line." Determined to make him jealous, she arranges for Phillip to discover her with another man when he returns. Phillip had intended to propose marriage to Anna, but changes his mind after discovering her "infidelity." Phillip and Anna eventually make up, and the film ends on a happy note. *Indiscreet* was the film version of the successful Broadway play *Kind Sir,* which starred Charles Boyer and Mary Martin.

In mid-October, 1958, Grant and Betsy Drake issued an abrupt statement to the press announcing their separation: "After careful consideration and long discussion, we have decided to live apart. We have had, and always will have, a deep love and respect for each other, but alas, our marriage has not brought us the happiness we fully expected and mutually desired. Since we have no children needful of our affection, it is, consequently, best that we separate for a while." They would remain separated for nearly four years. During that time, they visited one another periodically. Grant would travel to see her every year on her birthday from wherever on the globe he happened to be.

While separated from Betsy Drake, Grant underwent psychoanalysis. Part of his prescribed treatment required the use of LSD, the much publicized psychedelic drug of the 1960s. Grant considered the chemotherapeutic aspect of his treatment to be the most effective: "I know that all my life I've been going around in a fog. One day, after weeks of LSD, my last defense crumbled. To my delight, I found I had a tough inner core of strength. All my life I think I've been running from what I wanted most. I always felt my mother rejected me. Now I've developed a great compassion for my parents. And I love women, now. They are the mothers of the earth, so often imposed on by men. I've been through an experience that has completely changed me. It was horrendous. I had to face things about myself w never admitted, which I didn't know there. Now I know that I hurt every woman that I ever loved. Betsy and I have been separated for many months. When I went through [the LSD therapy] I found I loved her more than I'd ever imagined. Whether or not we ever get back together again, we shall always feel the same way about each other. But I could not have been a good husband to any woman. Well, now my attitude towards women is completely different. I do not intend to foul up any more lives. I am aware of my faults and I am ready to accept responsibilities and exchange tolerances."

Grant and Sophia Loren were re-united in 1958 in *Houseboat,* in which Grant plays Tom, the father of many children, including eight-year-old Robert Winston (Charles Herbert). Robert wanders off during a concert and meets Cinzia (Loren) and brings her home to meet "Daddie," who in turn asks her to stay as their housekeeper. Tom has a girlfriend (Martha Hyer), however, but he leaves her by the film's close for Cinzia. Aside from the romantic theme, there are many touching scenes between Grant and his children, especially one in which he is called upon to explain the hereafter. Reviewers considered *Houseboat* a successful, adult light comedy.

In 1959, Hitchcock again contacted Grant; he needed a leading man for *North by Northwest.* This film's complicated story centers about Roger Thornhill (Grant), a business executive mistaken for a secret agent by a ring of spies. Roger is kidnapped by the spy ring and forced into an alcoholic stupor. Next, they put him in an automobile, supposedly to drive to his death. Of course, he does not die; someone else does, but Roger is blamed for the death. Now, he has the police on his tail as well as the spy ring. In his anxious travels, he meets Eve

On location, but out of costume, for *The Pride and the Passion* (1957).

Grant and Ingrid Bergman, enjoy a conversational moment at a press conference in London, 1957.

(Above) During the filming of *Indiscreet* (1958), Grant and Ingrid Bergman stroll by two members of the Law Courts in Golden Lane, London.

(Right) Meeting Ingrid Bergman, an old friend, upon her arrival at the airport in London to film *Indiscreet* (1958) with Grant. Bergman and Italian director Roberto Rossellini had just broken up after a controversial romance.

Kendall (Eva Marie Saint) and learns that she is a government agent who has infiltrated the spy ring and is in much danger. Roger attempts a heroic rescue. He grasps her from the clutches of, and ultimately does away with, the leader of the spy ring (James Mason).

Operation Petticoat (1959) surprisingly was Grant's number one all-time money maker. Directed by Blake Edwards (who later became the mastermind behind Peter Sellers's "Pink Panther" series), it co-stars Tony Curtis as an assistant to Captain Sherman (Grant). Sherman is the skipper of a damaged submarine in Manila Bay who wishes to raise the vessel and get it to a dry dock to have it repaired. Curtis helps him by stealing from the mainland everything needed to raise the sub, but causes trouble by bringing two beautiful nurses (Dina Merrill and Joan O'Brien) on board.

In 1960, Grant starred in *The Grass Is Greener,* another lightweight movie. The story opens with Victor Rhyall (Grant), the Earl of Rhyall, and his wife Hilary (Deborah Kerr) in residence at stately Lynley Hall. A sightseer,

Grant and actress Eva Marie Saint about to board a plane for Chicago to film scenes from *North By Northwest* (1959).

Grant goes down the hatch of the submarine H.M.S. Narwhal in Finnart, Scotland. Grant was aboard the sub in connection with the filming of *Operation Petticoat* (1959).

A tourist (r.) in Moscow's Red Square, 1958. A Russian welcomes Grant with a handshake.

Charles Delacro (Robert Mitchum), meets and falls in love with Hilary. It all ends with a pistol duel between the rivals: Charles wounds Victor; Victor misses Charles; Hilary runs to her husband realizing, after all, how much she loves him.

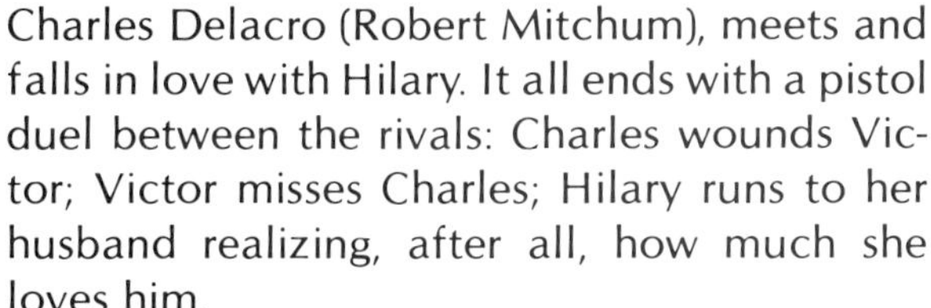

Grant's next endeavor was *That Touch of Mink* (1962), co-produced with Martin Melcher. Melcher's wife, Doris Day, co-stars. It is the story of Phillip Shayne (Grant), a wealthy bachelor with no interest in marriage and his unsuccessful pursuit of the virginal Miss Day. During the course of the film, he changes his mind about marrying, and at the end, they go off to enjoy a honeymoon in Bermuda.

On August 13, 1962, Betsy Drake obtained a divorce from Cary Grant. Love could not sustain or repair a marriage suffering in many irreconcilable ways. "He appeared to be bored with me," she said. "It was terribly frustrating to be married to Cary because he's a very self-sufficient man."

Grant had only kind words for Betsy: "She was good for me. I've never clearly resolved

Visiting Sophia Loren (r.) at the Cinecitta Film Studios, Rome, 1960. Grant's arm is around Sophia's younger sister Maria.

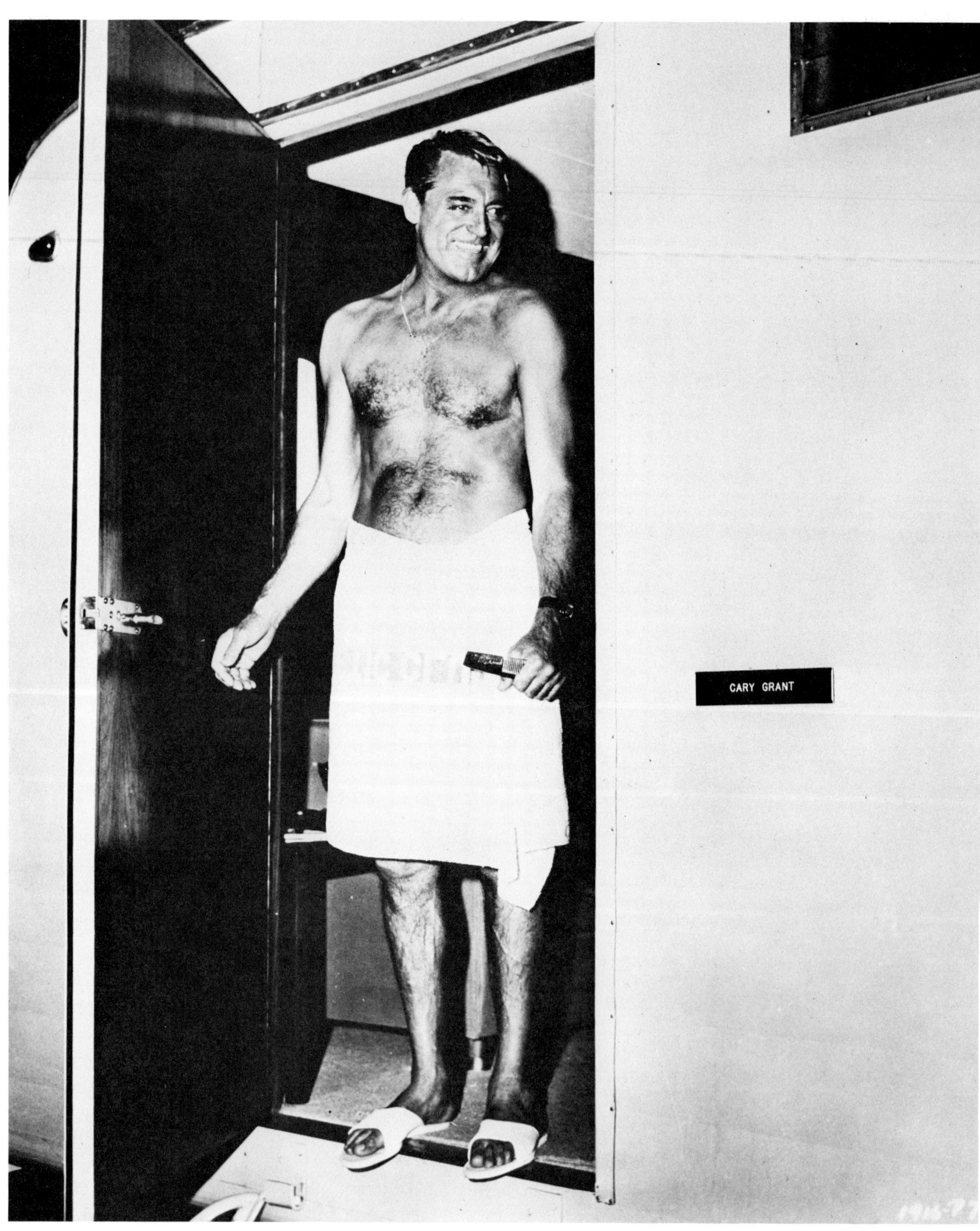

Preparing for a scene in *That Touch of Mink* (1962).

Publicity photograph, *That Touch Of Mink* (1962). Seated in the dugout with co-stars Grant and Doris Day are (l. to r.) New York Yankees Roger Maris, Mickey Mantle, and Yogi Berra.

why she and I parted. We lived together not as easily and contently as some, perhaps; yet, it seemed to me, happier than most. I owe a lot to Betsy. In each of my failed marriages, the woman deserved my love, but honestly, I had none to give. I didn't know how to love for the simple reason that I didn't know myself. I was racked with doubts, fears, and skepticism. I was unhappy with my past, dissatisfied with the present, and fearful of the future." Divorced for a third time, it was not surprising that Grant questioned whether it was in his constitution to sustain a loving, permanent relationship, and he returned to therapy.

Under psychiatric and LSD treatment, Grant discovered his capacity for happiness and contentment, and he delighted in his release from tensions and inner turmoils. "You've got to get over the blows your ego received in childhood. You have to learn how to forgive your parents the things they didn't know. And be grateful for what they did know. You have to use some deceit in this world to earn a living, but paradoxically, you will live longer, have a

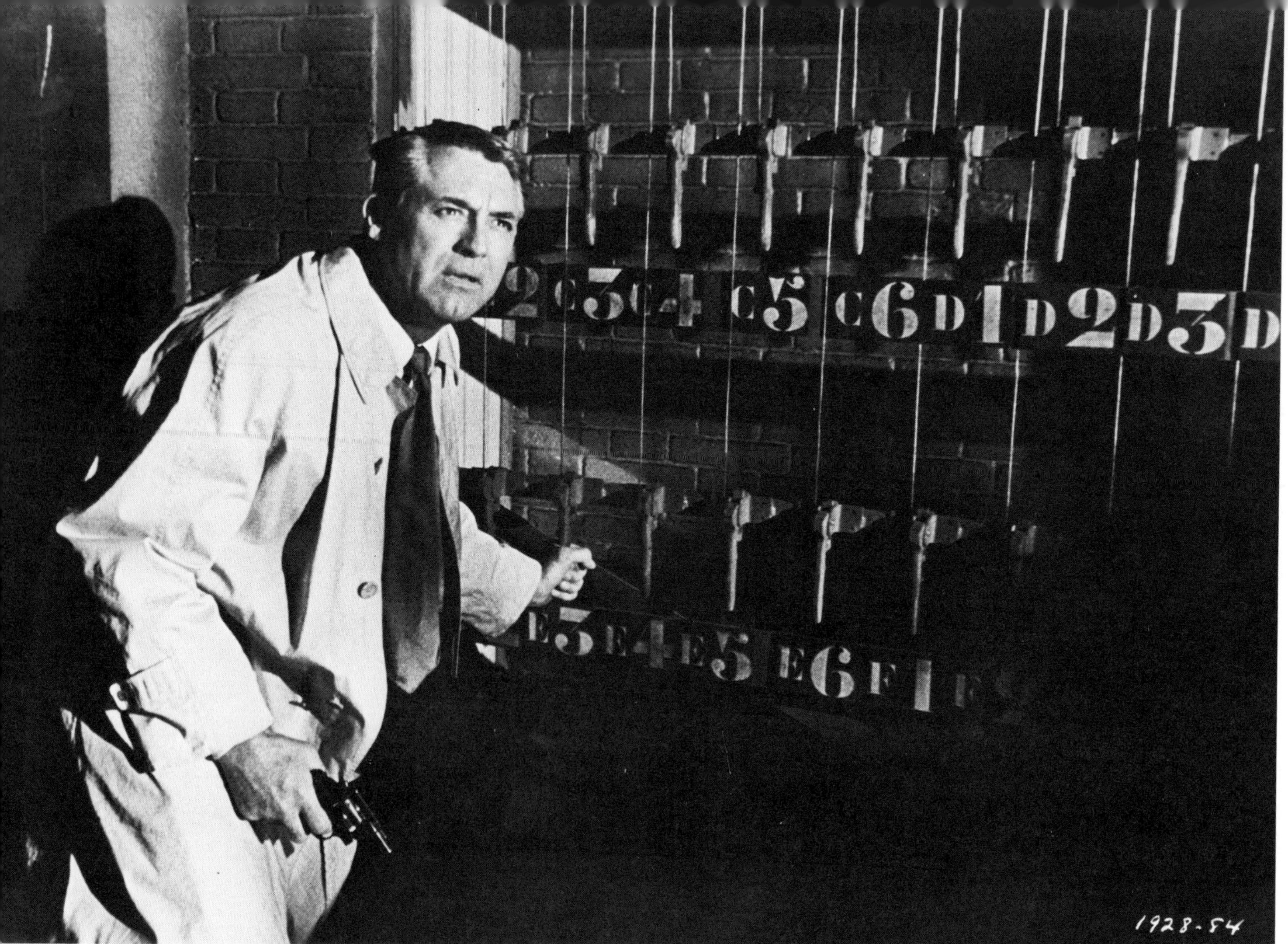

As Peter Joshua in *Charade* (1963).

better life and be more contented if you relax and be yourself."

Grant's new-found philosophy also led him to issue a list of "The Devastating Facts of Life" as he saw them:

> *Never do anyone a favor. It will make him feel inferior to you. Do someone a favor and you've probably made an enemy for life.
>
> *Have the good manners to wait until you are asked before offering an opinion. Once you are asked, say exactly what you think. You'll be misunderstood anyway, so you might as well taste the pleasures of honesty.
>
> *Don't expect to be rewarded if you do tell the truth.
>
> *Learn how to be unhappy.
>
> *Respect women because they are wiser than men.
>
> *Deplore bad taste and bad manners. Honesty is the best manners.
>
> *Deplore your mistakes, but don't expect to learn from them.
>
> *Suspect people. You can't rely on them.
>
> *Rely on yourself. There's no such

thing as bad luck.

At about this time, Grant met actress Dyan Cannon. He was fifty-nine years old, she, twenty-five. Her father was an insurance salesman in Tacoma, Washington, her mother, a housewife. Cannon had attended the University of Washinton for two years prior to beginning her stage and film career. Before flying to Paris to film *Charade* (1963) with Audrey Hepburn, Grant stopped off in Philadelphia to see Cannon in *The Fun Couple,* a play, perhaps on its way to Broadway, also starring Jane Fonda and Bradford Dillman.

Charade, directed by Stanley Donen, resembled the Hitchcock style. Regina Lambert (Audrey Hepburn) returns to Paris after a vacation and finds her home has been burglarized, stripped bare, and her husband has been murdered. Peter Joshua (Grant), a man she had met while away, volunteers to help her find the culprit. It turns out that Mr. Lambert had hidden away a quarter-of-a-million dollars before his demise. Thus, all of Lambert's "friends" are under suspicion. Even Joshua is considered a possible suspect. One by one, the dead man's cronies are done away with until at last Joshua saves Regina from certain death at the hands of a heretofore unsuspected character (Walter Matthau).

Filmed in 1964, *Father Goose* is a delightful story of Walter Ecklund (Grant), a hermit living in a hut on a deserted South Pacific island. He is persuaded by an Australian commander (Trevor Howard) to watch for Japanese forces that might mobilize for an attack on his country. Ecklund's assigned code name is "Mother Goose." He attempts to rescue another lookout on a nearby island, but he discovers his colleague is dead. He does find, however, eight stranded civilians. The lone adult among them (Leslie Caron) is a private tutor, the others are her students. He brings them back to his hut where they domesticate him, clean up his comfortable mess, and reorganize his life. At the end, Caron and Grant fall in love and are married by military radio.

Peter Stone contributed to the screenplay,

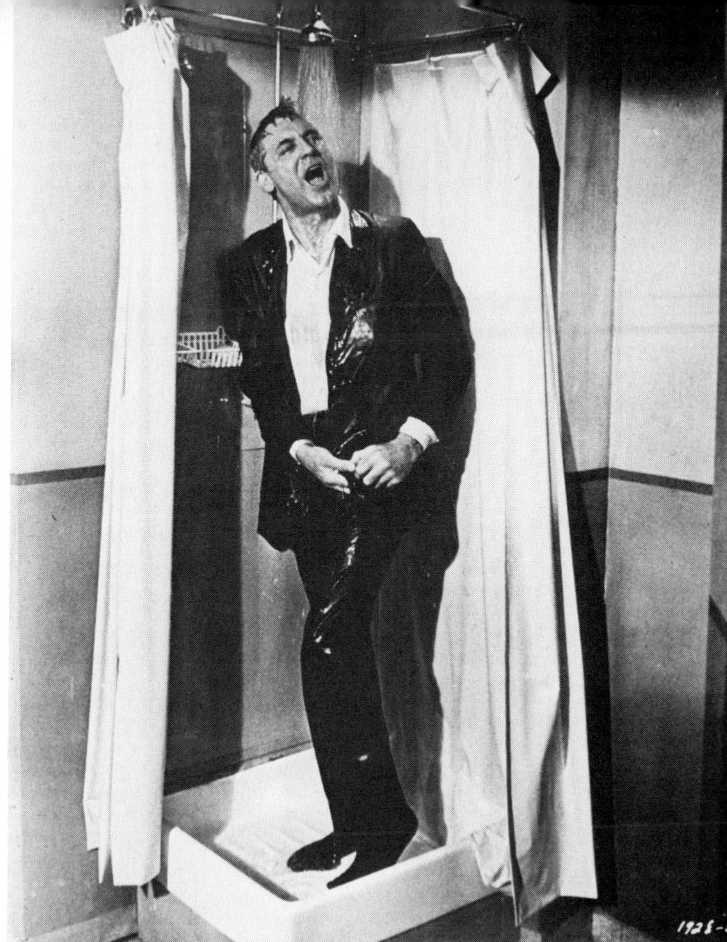

Getting doused in *Charade* (1963).

and when accepting his Academy Award for *Father Goose*, he offered his thanks to Grant. "Thank you, Cary," he said. "You keep winning these things for other people."

Father Goose was released in December, 1964. Earlier that year, Grant celebrated his sixtieth birthday. A reporter asked him to explain why he appeared so much younger than his years. Grant replied: "I don't try to follow a regular program. I ride [horses] a lot. I like to swim. I try to do what I want to do at the time. I don't eat many fatty foods, but I really don't know whether that's important or not. I eat only when I'm hungry, and read when I'm not. Sometimes I don't sleep for three days. Other times I go to sleep for the whole weekend. Life is just an occupation of time. It's all a matter of what you do between getting up and going to bed."

Then he was asked to speculate on the future: "Right now, man is intent on getting to

Actor Sidney Poitier drops in on the set of *Father Goose* (1964). Co-stars Leslie Caron and Grant (r.) join in the conversation between Poitier and director Ralph Nelson (l.).

(Above) Grant and Leslie Caron (both r.) turn real-life heroes during filming of *Father Goose* (1964) after an 8-foot dinghy with 7 children aboard capsized. At left is assistant director Mike Moder and one of the children, Verina Greenlaw.

Mars before we bust this planet up. The Earth will probably be another sun one day, sustaining life on another planet through its radioactivity. Machines will take over for human beings, perhaps. After all, electronic machines are the collective results of the thoughts in many men's minds and therefore have the power of many men's minds. As a result, sooner or later, they should be able to find a way to reproduce themselves."

The reporter asking the question was female. "There, you see? You're a woman and can't conceive of this. Women particularly hang on to their neuroses and think there can be no reproduction without emotion. But is emotion necessary for reproduction? A virus reproduces itself, and it not only has no emotion, but no mind. So a brilliant machine?... These themes represent the cyclical nature of things, you just go along with them. And this kind of thinking fascinates me as acting fascinates me."

In July, 1965, a half-year after the release of *Father Goose,* Grant married Dyan Cannon in Las Vegas. The press did not learn of the ceremony until the couple had left for England where Grant introduced Cannon to his mother.

Cary Grant's seventy-second and final film of his thirty-four-year Hollywood career was shot in early 1966. *Walk, Don't Run* (1966) is an apt film to close Grant's career. It is a light comedy about a British industrialist in Tokyo during the Olympic Games. As a handsome, fatherly sort, Grant plays Cupid to Samantha Eggar and Jim Hutton. It is as if Grant is acknowledging the passage of time and bowing to Nature. I

With Sharyl Locke (above) and Leslie Caron in *Father Goose* (1964).

Grant and Angie Dickenson flash smiles as they receive awards as "Star of the Year" and "Most Exciting New Star," respectively, at the Americana Hotel, N.Y., 1963.

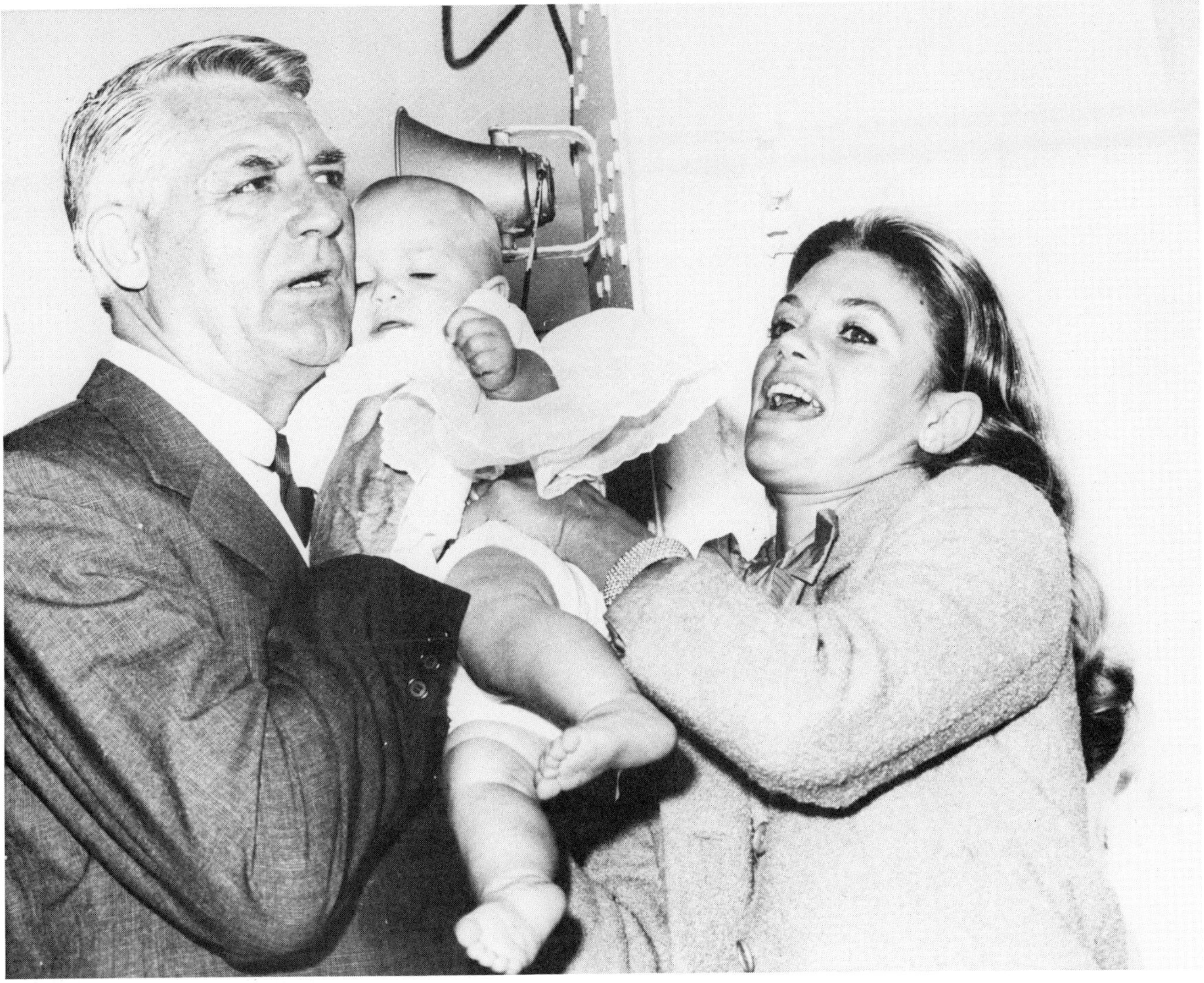

Grant, his fourth wife, actress Dyan Cannon, and their daughter Jennifer, Grant's only child, 1966.

can't play romantic leads anymore, he seems to be saying, but I don't want to. So many times it was he who won the beauty; he who, no matter how far-fetched, complicated, or unlikely the romance, ended up marrying the object of his desire. But now Cary Grant was through winning the woman and through making pictures.

In another sense, though, his life had just begun. Grant's long-dreamed-about, first child arrived on February 26, 1966. She was named Jennifer and weighed four pounds, eight ounces at birth. Grant was ecstatic: "I've waited all my life hoping for children, and when you've waited for such a long time, you hope like mad that everything will work out all right. In my case, I knew the birth of my baby was the chance of a dream coming true. It's never too late to become a parent." He, Dyan, and Jennifer then flew to Bristol, England, to see Mrs. Leach. "Presenting Jennifer to my mother was the proudest moment of my life," Grant later

Rosalind Russell bestows a kiss on Grant after he presented her with the Stock Theaters' Straw Hat Award, May 29, 1975.

told reporters.

In December of 1966, Dyan Cannon requested and was granted a separation from Grant. He tried to effect a reconciliation, but she declined. Grant contested her divorce suit and much private information became public. Cannon charged that Grant experienced screaming fits while "tripping" on LSD and requested that his visitation with their daughter be severely limited. The judge denied the request: "The evidence shows that Mr. Grant is no longer using LSD, and he appears to be a loving, devoted father. He should be entitled to adequate visitation rights. If his conduct is not as it should be, then the plaintiff may return to court."

For some time following their divorce, Cannon and Grant had no contact whatsoever with each other, but gradually the bitterness wore off. "Jennifer is my life today," says Grant. "I plan around her, where she is, when I may have her." He has absolutely ruled out the possibility of making another picture. "I've had it. I can't think of going back and listening to all that deplorable conversation on the set and go tripping over all those cables."

On Tuesday, April 7, 1970, Grant was awarded his first Oscar. Presented by Frank Sinatra, the gold inscription read: "To Cary Grant for his unique mastery of the art of screen acting with the respect and affection of his colleagues." Grant thanked the audience for their thunderous standing ovation and, in the course of his speech, said: "Probably no greater honor can come to a man than the respect of his colleagues."

Grant now works as a member of the board of directors of Rayette-Faberge, and he is still as outspoken as ever. "I am often troubled by parents who come up to me and say 'My children will kill me if I don't get your autograph.' I'm troubled by such peculiar family relationships. It gives me indigestion. One woman approached me and said, 'You're so wonderful. You make me shake.' 'You make yourself shake,' I told her. Anyway, autograph collecting is just a racket. Those people will beat the hell out of you just to get some scribbling on a scrap of paper. If you stop and sign, you feel like a silly fool. There you are in the middle of the sidewalk, surrounded by rude, yelling, wriggling people and writing away like crazy."

Grant on looking young and the subconscious: "I'm sick and tired of being questioned about why I look young for my age and how I keep trim. I'm not at all sure I look young for my age, but even if I did, why should the idiots make so much of it? Why don't they emulate it rather than gasp about it? The subconscious holds all knowledge, I believe. If you really think thin, you'll get there. You won't need a diet or medical plan. The subconscious will tell you what to eat or pass up. It's a funny thing, but when I was young and a popular star, I'd meet a girl with a guy, and maybe she'd say something nice about me, and then the guy would say, 'Yeah, but I hear he's really a fag.' Now, in fact, the guy is doing me a favor. Number one, he's expressed an insecurity about the girl. Number two, he has provoked curiosity about me in her. Number three, that girl zeros in on my bed to find out for herself, and the result is that the guy has created the exact situation he wanted to avoid."

Grant holds his ear as Danny Kaye gives out with an ear-splitting whistle at a party at the Waldorf Astoria, N.Y., 1975.

On his life today: "Oh, I'd prefer to be younger and know what I know today and be able to apply it to life in every aspect, but I am very happy. I don't put a great deal of effort into my work for Faberge. I get up in the morning, go to bed at night, and occupy myself as best I can in between. I do what I want, when I want. Once, in St. Louis, I knew a fellow who ran a whorehouse because it made him happy. Well, I do what makes me happy."

Beside New York's East River, 1974. Grant was taking part in ceremonies held to note that portions of New York's East Side are built on rubble shipped from Bristol, England, Grant's birthplace, during World War II.

Nearly a generation ago, Grant described his plan for professional success. He began by analogizing the Hollywood fame game to a particular kind of crowded trolley car: "It's a streetcar, the kind where you get on in the rear and slowly make your way forward—where the exit is located. The car runs on a circular track, starting nowhere and arriving nowhere. The point is to keep it moving, it doesn't matter where. It's a terrifyingly hard job to get aboard in the first place. And once you've bucked and line-plunged your way to a handhold inside the stuffed car, you have to fight with fang and claw to keep from being jarred loose or pushed off into Oblivion Street. You see, chivalry has no place on the street marked Fame. There's no room for it. Your fellow passengers are intent on gouging out your eyes and busting your ribs and stamping on your feet. If a woman gets in your way, correct Hollywood etiquette is to slug her before she slugs you. Any display of manners marks you for a sap and a sissy, therefore ineligible for the long ride. Some easygoing chumps, too soft-hearted to play the Fame game, have been bounced off the back of the car before they had a chance to pay their fare. Others have been knocked through a window as they paused to apologize to somebody for inadvertently breaking an arm. If you're strong, ruthless, and lucky enough to get a seat, the trick is to glue yourself to it and sit tight until some tougher mug shoves you up toward the front. One day I was walking along on my stilts, minding my own business, and I noticed a streetcar transfer lying on the sidewalk. I climbed down, parked my stilts, and got on the car. I've been riding ever since."

2 THE FILMS OF CARY GRANT

1932 **THIS IS THE NIGHT** (Paramount). Director, Frank Tuttle. Cast included: Irving Bacon, Lily Damita, Claire Dodd, Charles Ruggles, Thelma Todd, and Roland Young. Screenplay, George Marion, Jr.; from a play by Avery Hopwood.

1932 **MERRILY WE GO TO HELL** (Paramount). Director, Dorothy Arzner. Cast included: Adrianne Allen, Richard "Skeets" Gallagher, Fredric March, Sylvia Sidney, and Kent Taylor. Screenplay, Edwin Justus Mayer; from the novel by Cleo Lucas.

1932 **SINNERS IN THE SUN** (Paramount). Director, Alexander Hall. Cast included: Adrienne Ames, Walter Byron, Carole Lombard, Chester Morris, and Alison Skipworth. Screenplay, Samuel Hoffenstein, Vincent Lawrence, and Waldemar Young; based on a story by Mildred Cram.

1932 **DEVIL AND THE DEEP** (Paramount). Director, Marion Gering. Cast included: Tallulah Bankhead, Juliette Compton, Gary Cooper, Henry Kolker, Charles Laughton, Paul Porcasi, and Kent Taylor. Screenplay, Benn W. Levy; adapted from a story by Harry Hervey.

With Thelma Todd, Roland Young (c.), and Charles Ruggles in *This Is The Night* (1932).

With Sylvia Sidney and Fredric March (r.) in *Merrily We Go To Hell* (1932).

With Carole Lombard in *Sinners In The Sun* (1932).

With Charles Laughton in *Devil And The Deep* (1932).

With Marlene Dietrich in *Blonde Venus* (1932).

1932 **HOT SATURDAY** (Paramount). Director, Wiliam A. Seiter. Cast included: Lillian Bond, Nancy Carroll, William Collier, Sr., Jane Darwell, Randolph Scott, Grady Sutton, and Edward Woods. Screenplay, Seton I. Miller; adapted from the novel by Harvey Fergusson.

1932 **BLONDE VENUS** (Paramount). Director, Josef von Sternberg. Cast included: Cecil Cunningham, Marlene Dietrich, Hattie McDaniel, Herbert Marshall, Dickie Moore, and Sidney Toler. Screenplay, Jules Furthman and S. K. Lauren; from a story by Josef von Sternberg.

1932 **MADAME BUTTERFLY** (Paramount). Director, Marion Gering. Cast included: Helen Jerome Eddy, Irving Pichel, Charles Ruggles, and Sylvia Sidney. Screenplay, Joseph Lovett and Joseph Moncure March; from a story by John Luther Long and a play by David Belasco.

(Above) With Nancy Carroll in *Hot Saturday* (1932).

(Below) With Sheila Terry (c.) in *Madame Butterfly* (1932).

(Above) With Mae West in *She Done Him Wrong* (1933).

1933 **SHE DONE HIM WRONG** (Paramount). Director, Lowell Sherman. Cast included: Louise Beavers, Noah Beery, Sr., Rochelle Hudson, Fuzzy Knight, David Landau, Owen Moore, Rafaela Ottiano, Gilbert Roland, and Mae West. Screenplay, John Bright and Harvey Thew; based on a play by Mae West.

(Above right) With Nancy Carroll in *The Woman Accused* (1933).

(Right) With Fredric March (l.) in *The Eagle And The Hawk* (1933).

1933 **THE WOMAN ACCUSED** (Paramount). Director, Paul Sloane. Cast included: Louis Calhern, Nancy Carroll, John Halliday, Jack LaRue, John Lodge, and Irving Pichel. Screenplay, Bayard Veiller; taken from magazine serial by Gertrude Atherton, Polan Banks, Vicki Baum, Irvin S. Cobb, Vina Delmar, Zane Grey, Rupert Hughes, Sophie Kerr, J. P. McEvoy, and Ursula Parrott.

1933 **THE EAGLE AND THE HAWK** (Paramount). Director, Stuart Walker. Cast included: Carole Lombard, Fredric March, Jack Oakie, Sir Guy Standing. Screenplay, Seton I. Miller and Bogart Rogers; from a story by John Monk Saunders.

With Jack LaRue (l.), Benita Hume, and Roscoe Karns (r.) in *Gambling Ship* (1933).

1933 **GAMBLING SHIP** (Paramount). Directors, Louis Gasnier and Max Marcin. Cast included: Glenda Farrell, Benita Hume, Roscoe Karns, Jack LaRue, and Arthur Vinton. Screenplay, Max Marcin and Seton I. Miller; from a story by Peter Ruric and an adaptation by Claude Binyon.

1933 **I'M NO ANGEL** (Paramount). Director, Wesley Ruggles. Cast included: Edward Arnold, Ralf Harolde, Russell Hopton, Gertrude Michael, Dorothy Peterson, Gregory Ratoff, Kent Taylor, and Mae West. Screenplay, Lowell Brentano and Mae West.

(Above right) With Mae West in *I'm No Angel* (1933).

(Right) As the Mock Turtle in *Alice In Wonderland* (1933), With Charlotte Henry (c.) and William Austin (l.).

1933 **ALICE IN WONDERLAND** (Paramount). Director, Norman Z. McLeod. Cast included: Richard Arlen, Gary Cooper, Leon Errol, Louise Fazenda, W. C. Fields, Charlotte Henry, Sterling Holloway, Edward Everett Horton, Baby LeRoy, Mae Marsh, Jack Oakie, Edna May Oliver, May Robson, Charles Ruggles, Alison Skipworth, Ned Sparks, Jacqueline Wells (Julie Bishop). Screenplay, Joseph L. Mankiewicz and William Cameron Menzies; adapted from the story by Lewis Carroll.

1489-6.

With Genevieve Tobin (l.) and Helen Mack (r.) in *Kiss And Make-Up* (1934).

(Above left) With Sylvia Sidney in *Thirty-Day Princess* (1934).

(Left) With Loretta Young and Etienne Girardot (r.) in *Born To Be Bad* (1934).

1934 **THIRTY-DAY PRINCESS** (Paramount). Director, Marion Gering. Cast included: Edward Arnold, Vince Barnett, Edgar Norton, Sylvia Sidney, and Henry Stephenson. Screenplay, Frank Partos and Preston Sturges; based on a story by Clarence Buddington Kelland.

1934 **BORN TO BE BAD** (United Artists). Director, Lowell Sherman. Cast included: Marion Burns, Harry Green, Russell Hopton, Jackie Kelk, Andrew Tombes, Henry Travers, and Loretta Young. Screenplay, Ralph Graves.

1934 **KISS AND MAKE-UP** (Paramount). Director, Harlan Thompson. Cast included: Edward Everett Horton, Helen Mack, Mona Maris, Clara Lou (Ann) Sheridan, Genevieve Tobin, Jacqueline Wells (Julie Bishop), and Toby Wing. Screenplay, George Marion, Jr. and Harlan Thompson; from a play by Stephen Bekeffi and an adaptation by Jane Hinton.

With Nydia Westman in *Ladies Should Listen* (1934).

1934 **LADIES SHOULD LISTEN** (Paramount). Director, Frank Tuttle. Cast included: Charles Arnt, George Barbier, Frances Drake, Edward Everett Horton, Rosita Moreno, Clara Lou (Ann) Sheridan, and Nydia Westman. Screenplay, Claude Binyon and Frank Butler; based on a play by Guy Bolton and Alfred Savoir.

1934 **ENTER MADAME** (Paramount). Director, Elliott Nugent. Cast included: Frank Albertson, Elissa Landi, Sharon Lynn, Lynne Overman, Cecilia Parker, and Clara Lou (Ann) Sheridan. Screenplay, Charles Brackett and Gladys Lehman; from a play by Dorothea Donn-Byrne and Gilda Varesi.

With Linne Overman (l.) in *Enter Madame* (1934).

With Myrna Loy in *Wings In The Dark* (1935).

With Jamison Thomas in *The Last Outpost* (1935).

1935 **WINGS IN THE DARK** (Paramount). Director, James Flood. Cast included: Hobart Cavanaugh, Bert Hanlon, Russell Hopton, Dean Jagger, Roscoe Karns, and Myrna Loy. Screenplay, Jack Kirkland and Frank Partos; from a story by Philip D. Hurn and Neil Shipman, as adapted by Dale Van Every.

1935 **THE LAST OUTPOST** (Paramount). Directors, Charles Barton and Louis Gasnier. Cast included: Kathleen Burke, Gertrude Michael, Claude Rains, and Colin Tapley. Screenplay, Philip MacDonald; based on a story by F. Britten, as adapted by Charles Brackett and Frank Partos.

(Left) With Katharine Hepburn in *Sylvia Scarlett* (1936).

1936 **SYLVIA SCARLETT** (RKO). Director, George Cukor, Cast included: Brian Aherne, Edmund Gwenn, Katherine Hepburn, Dennie Moore, and Natalie Paley. Screenplay, John Collier, Mortimer Offner, and Gladys Unger; from the novel by Compton Mackenzie.

1936 **BIG BROWN EYES** (Paramount). Director, Raoul Walsh. Cast included: Alan Baxter, Joan Bennett, Douglas Fowley, Marjorie Gateson, Isabel Jewell, Lloyd Nolan, and Walter Pidgeon. Screenplay, Bert Hanlon and Raoul Walsh; adapted from short stories by James Edward Grant.

(Below) With Joan Bennett in *Big Brown Eyes* (1936).

With Jean Harlow and Franchot Tone (r.) in *Suzy* (1936).

1936 **SUZY** (MGM). Director, George Fitzmaurice. Cast included: Inez Courtney, Jean Harlow, Benita Hume, Stanley Morner (Dennis Morgan), Una O'Conner, Lewis Stone, and Franchot Tone. Screenplay, Alan Campbell, Lenore Coffee, Horace Jackson, and Dorothy Parker; from a novel by Herbert Gorman.

(Above) With Joan Bennett (rear) in *Wedding Present* (1936).

(Below left) With Mary Brian in *The Amazing Quest Of Ernest Bliss* (1936).

1936 **WEDDING PRESENT** (Paramount). Director, Richard Wallace. Cast included: George Bancroft, Joan Bennett, Edward Brophy, Inez Courtney, William Demarest, Gene Lockhart, and Conrad Nagel. Screenplay, Joseph Anthony; based on a story by Paul Gallico.

1936 **THE AMAZING QUEST OF ERNEST BLISS** (Grand National). (Released in the U.S. in 1937 as **ROMANCE AND RICHES;** subsequently re-released by Astor Pictures as **AMAZING ADVENTURE.** Alternate title in England: **A RICH YOUNG MAN.**) Director, Alfred Zeisler. Cast included: Mary Brian, Peter Gawthorne, Henry Kendall, and John Turnbull. Screenplay, John L. Balderston; adapted from a story by E. Phillips Oppenheim.

(Above) With (l. to r.) Emma Dunn, Grace Moore, and George Pearce in *When You're in Love* (1937).

(Below) With Frances Farmer in *The Toast Of New York* (1937).

1937 **WHEN YOU'RE IN LOVE** (Columbia). Director, Robert Riskin. Cast included: Luis Alberni, Catherine Doucet, Emma Dunn, Aline MacMahon, Thomas Mitchell, Grace Moore, and Henry Stephenson. Screenplay, Robert Riskin; from a story by Ethel Hill and Cedric Worth.

1937 **THE TOAST OF NEW YORK** (RKO). Director, Rowland V. Lee. Cast included: Edward Arnold, Frances Farmer, Billy Gilbert, Clarence Kolb, Thelma Leeds, Donald Meek, and Jack Oakie. Screenplay, Dudley Nichols, Joel Sayre, and John Twist; based on a book by Bouck White and a story by Matthew Josephson.

With Katharine Hepburn in *Bringing Up Baby* (1938).

1937 **TOPPER** (MGM). Director, Norman Z. McLeod. Cast included: Constance Bennett, Billie Burke, Hedda Hopper, Arthur Lake, Alan Mowbray, Eugene Pallette, Virginia Sale, and Roland Young. Screenplay, Eric Hatch, Jack Jevne, and Eddie Moran; from the novel by Thorne Smith.

1937 **THE AWFUL TRUTH** (Columbia). Director, Leo McCarey. Cast included: Ralph Bellamy, Cecil Cunningham, Alexander D'Arcy, Esther Dale, Irene Dunne, Mary Forbes, Molly Lamont, and Mr. Smith ("Asta" of the *Thin Man* series). Screenplay, Vina Delmar; adapted from a play by Arthur Richman.

(Above left) With J. Farrell McDonald (l.) and Constance Bennett in *Topper* (1937).

1938 **BRINGING UP BABY** (RKO). Director, Howard Hawks. Cast included: Tala Birell, Walter Catlett, Fritz Feld, Barry Fitzgerald, Katharine Hepburn, May Robson, and Charles Ruggles. Screenplay, Dudley Nichols and Hagar Wilde; from a story by Wilde.

(Left) With Irene Dunne and "Asta" in *The Awful Truth* (1937).

With Doris Nolan (l.) and Katharine Hepburn (r.) in *Holiday* (1938).

1938 **HOLIDAY** (Columbia). Director, George Cukor. Cast included: Lew Ayres, Binnie Barnes, Henry Daniell, Jean Dixon, Katharine Hepburn, Edward Everett Horton, Henry Kolker, and Doris Nolan. Screenplay, Sidney Buchman and Donald Ogden Stewart; based on the play by Philip Barry.

(Above right) With Victor McLaglen (c.) and Douglas Fairbanks, Jr. (r.) in *Gunga Din* (1939).

(Right) With Allyn Joslyn (c.), Jean Arthur, Sig Rumann, and Thomas Mitchell (r.) in *Only Angels Have Wings* (1939).

1939 **GUNGA DIN** (RKO). Director, George Stevens. Cast included: Eduardo Ciannelli, Douglas Fairbanks, Jr., Joan Fontaine, Sam Jaffe, Montagu Love, and Victor McLaglen. Screenplay, Fred Guiol and Joel Sayre; from a story by Ben Hecht and Charles MacArthur, suggested by Rudyard Kipling's poem.

1939 **ONLY ANGELS HAVE WINGS** (Columbia). Director, Howard Hawks. Cast included: Jean Arthur, Donald Barry, Richard Barthelmess, Noah Beery, Jr., John Carroll, Rita Hayworth, Allyn Joslyn, Victor Kilian, and Thomas Mitchell. Screenplay, Jules Furthman; based on a story by Howard Hawks.

With Carole Lombard in *In Name Only* (1939).

(Below) With Rosalind Russell in *His Girl Friday* (1940).

1939 **IN NAME ONLY** (RKO). Director, John Cromwell. Cast included: Katharine Alexander, Charles Coburn, Kay Francis, Peggy Ann Garner, Jonathan Hale, Carole Lombard, and Helen Vinson. Screenplay, Richard Sherman; adapted from a novel by Bessie Breuer.

1940 **HIS GIRL FRIDAY** (Columbia). Director, Howard Hawks. Cast included: Ralph Bellamy, Cliff Edwards, Billy Gilbert, Porter Hall, Frank Jenks, Roscoe Karns, Clarence Kolb, Gene Lockhart, Helen Mack, Marion Martin, John Qualen, Rosalind Russell, and Regis Toomey. Screenplay, Charles Lederer; based on a play by Ben Hecht and Charles MacArthur.

1940 **MY FAVORITE WIFE** (RKO). Director, Garson Kanin. Cast included: Granville Bates, Scotty Beckett, Irene Dunne, Donald MacBride, Gail Patrick, Ann Shoemaker, and Randolph Scott. Screenplay, Bella and Samuel Spewack; from a story by Leo McCarey and the Spewacks.

As Nick in *My Favorite Wife* (1940).

(Above) With (l. to r.) Martha Scott, Cedric Hardwicke, and Rita Quigley in *The Howards Of Virginia* (1940).

1940 **THE HOWARDS OF VIRGINIA** (Columbia). Director, Frank Lloyd. Cast included: Richard Alden (Tom Drake), Irving Bacon, Richard Carlson, Cedric Hardwicke, Alan Marshal, Anne Revere, Elizabeth Risdon, and Martha Scott. Screenplay, Sidney Buchman; adapted from a novel by Elizabeth Page.

1940 **THE PHLADELPHIA STORY** (MGM). Director, George Cukor. Cast included: Henry Daniell, John Halliday, Katharine Hepburn, John Howard, Ruth Hussey, Mary Nash, James Stewart, Virginia Weidler, and Roland Young. Screenplay, Donald Ogden Stewart; based on the play by Philip Barry.

(Above right) With Katharine Hepburn and James Stewart (r.) in *The Philadelphia Story* (1940).

(Right) With Irene Dunne and Grady Sutton (r.) in *Penny Serenade* (1941).

1941 **PENNY SERENADE** (Columbia). Director, George Stevens. Cast included: Beulah Bondi, Edgar Buchanan, Ann Doran, Irene Dunne, and Eva Lee Kuney. Screenplay, Morrie Ryskind; from a story by Martha Cheavens.

With Joan Fontaine in *Suspicion* (1941).

(Above) With Jean Arthur in *The Talk Of The Town* (1942).

(Above right) With Ginger Rogers in *Once Upon A Honeymoon* (1942).

1941 **SUSPICION** (RKO). Director, Alfred Hitchcock. Cast included: Heather Angel, Nigel Bruce, Leo G. Carroll, Joan Fontaine, Cedric Hardwicke, Isabel Jeans, and Dame May Whitty. Screenplay, Joan Harrison, Samson Raphaelson, and Alma Reville; based on a novel by Francis Iles.

1942 **THE TALK OF THE TOWN** (Columbia). Director, George Stevens. Cast included: Jean Arthur, Edgar Buchanan, Ronald Colman, Charles Dingle, Emma Dunn, Glenda Farrell, and Rex Ingram. Screenplay, Sidney Buchanan and Irwin Shaw.

1942 **ONCE UPON A HONEYMOON** (RKO). Director, Leo McCarey. Cast included: Albert Basserman, Ferike Boros, Albert Dekker, Ginger Rogers, and Walter Slezak. Screenplay, Sheridan Gibney; adapted from a story by Gibney and Leo McCarey.

With Laraine Day in *Mr. Lucky* (1943).

1943 **MR. LUCKY** (RKO). Director, H.C. Potter, Cast included: Florence Bates, Charles Bickford, Alan Carney, Gladys Cooper, Laraine Day, Kay Johnson, J.M. Kerrigan, Walter Kingsford, Vladimir Sokoloff, Henry Stephenson, and Paul Stewart. Screenplay, Milton Holmes and Adrian Scott.

1944 **DESTINATION TOKYO** (Warner Bros.). Director, Delmer Daves. Cast included: Warner Anderson, Dane Clark, Faye Emerson, John Forsythe, John Garfield, Alan Hale, Robert Hutton, William Prince, John Ridgely, and Tom Tully. Screenplay, Delmar Daves and Albert Maltz; from a story by Steve Fisher.

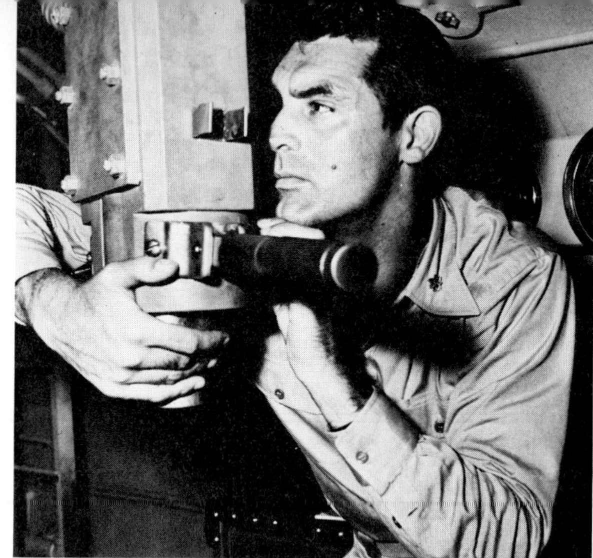

As Captain Cassidy in *Destination Tokyo* (1944).

1944 **ONCE UPON A TIME** (Columbia). Director, Alexander Hall. Cast included: Janet Blair, William Demarest, Ted Donaldson. Howard Freeman, and James Gleason. Screenplay, Lewis Meltzer and Oscar Paul; based on an adaptation by Irving Fineman, from a story by Norman Corwin and Lucille Fletcher Herrmann.

1944 **ARSENIC AND OLD LACE** (Warner Bros.). Director, Frank Capra. Cast included: Jean Adair, John Alexander, Jack Carson, James Gleason, Edward Everett Horton, Josephine Hall, Priscilla Lane, Peter Lorre, Raymond Massey, and Grant Mitchell. Screenplay, Julius J. and Philip G. Epstein; adapted from the play by Joseph Kesselring.

With William Austin (l.) and Torben Meyer (c.) in *Once Upon A Time* (1944).

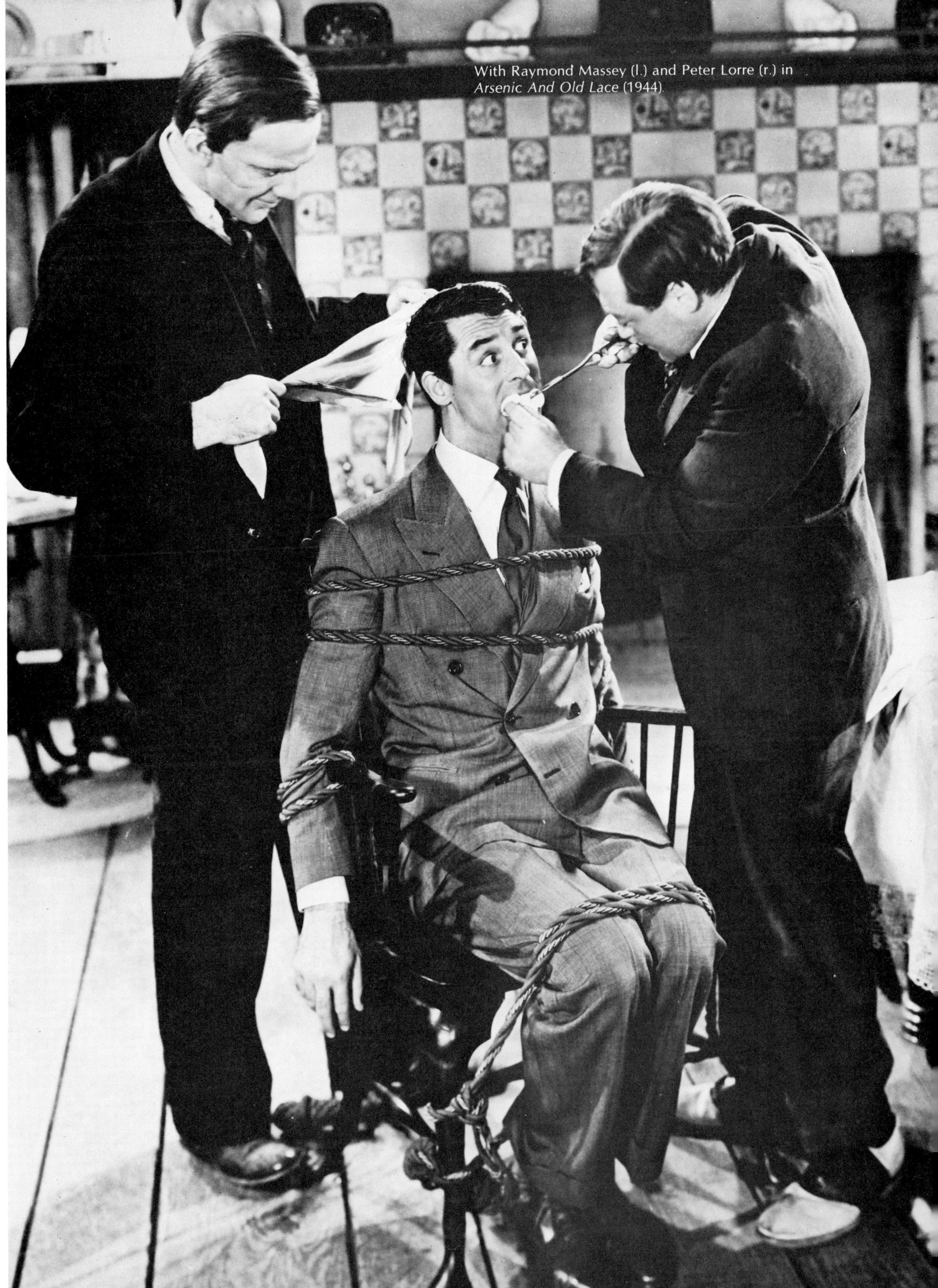

With Raymond Massey (l.) and Peter Lorre (r.) in *Arsenic And Old Lace* (1944).

(Left) As Ernie Mott in *None But The Lonely Heart* (1944).

(Right) With (l. to r.) Ingrid Bergman, Leopoldine Konstantin, and Claude Rains in *Notorious* (1946).

(Below left) With Alexis Smith in *Night And Day* (1946).

1944 **NONE BUT THE LONELY HEART** (RKO). Director, Clifford Odets. Cast included: Ethel Barrymore, Roman Bohnen, George Coulouris, June Duprez, Dan Duryea, Barry Fitzgerald, and Jane Wyatt. Screenplay, Clifford Odets; from a novel by Richard Llewellyn.

1946 **NIGHT AND DAY** (Warner Bros.). Director, Michael Curtiz. Cast included: Eve Arden, Victor Francen, Alan Hale, Dorothy Malone, Mary Martin, Selena Royle, Ginny Simms, Alexis Smith, Monty Wooley, and Jane Wyman. Screenplay, William Bowers, Charles Hoffman, and Leo Townsend; based on the life of Cole Porter.

1946 **NOTORIOUS** (RKO). Director, Alfred Hitchcock. Cast included: Ingrid Bergman, Louis Calhern, Leopoldine Konstantin, Moroni Olsen, Claude Rains, Reinhold Schunzel, and Ivan Triesault. Screenplay, Ben Hecht.

(Above) With (l. to r.) Myrna Loy, Veda Ann Borg, Don Beddoe, and Carol Hughes in *The Bachelor And The Bobby-Soxer* (1947).

1947 **THE BACHELOR AND THE BOBBY-SOXER** (RKO). Director, Irving Reis. Cast included: Don Beddoe, Vida Ann Borg, Ray Collins, Harry Davenport, Myrna Loy, Johnny Sands, Shirley Temple, and Rudy Vallee. Screenplay, Sidney Sheldon.

(Above) With David Niven (l.) and Loretta Young in *The Bishop's Wife* (1947).

(Below left) With Myrna Loy in *Mr. Blandings Builds His Dream House* (1948).

1947 **THE BISHOP'S WIFE** (RKO). Director, Henry Koster. Cast included: Gladys Cooper, James Gleason, Sara Haden, Elsa Lanchester, David Niven, Monty Wooley, and Loretta Young. Screenplay, Leonardo Bercovici and Robert E. Sherwood; from the novel by Robert Nathan.

1948 **MR. BLANDINGS BUILDS HIS DREAM HOUSE** (RKO). Director, H.C. Potter. Cast included: Louise Beavers, Reginald Denny, Melvyn Douglas, Connie Marshall, Sharyn Moffett, Myrna Loy, and Lurene Tuttle. Screenplay, Melvin Frank and Norman Panama; adapted from a novel by Eric Hodgins.

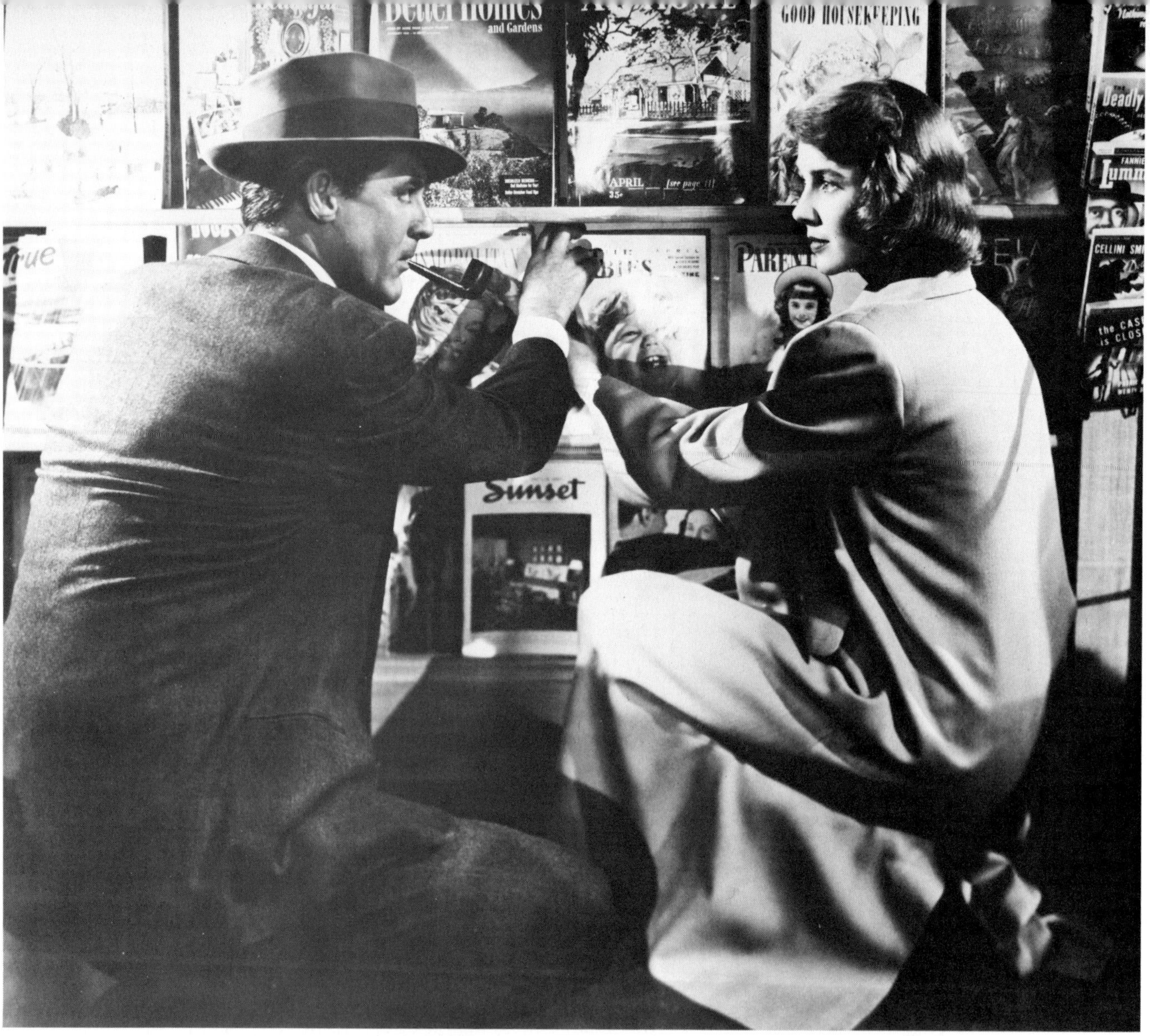
Better Homes
and Gardens
GOOD HOUSEKEEPING
APRIL
Sunset

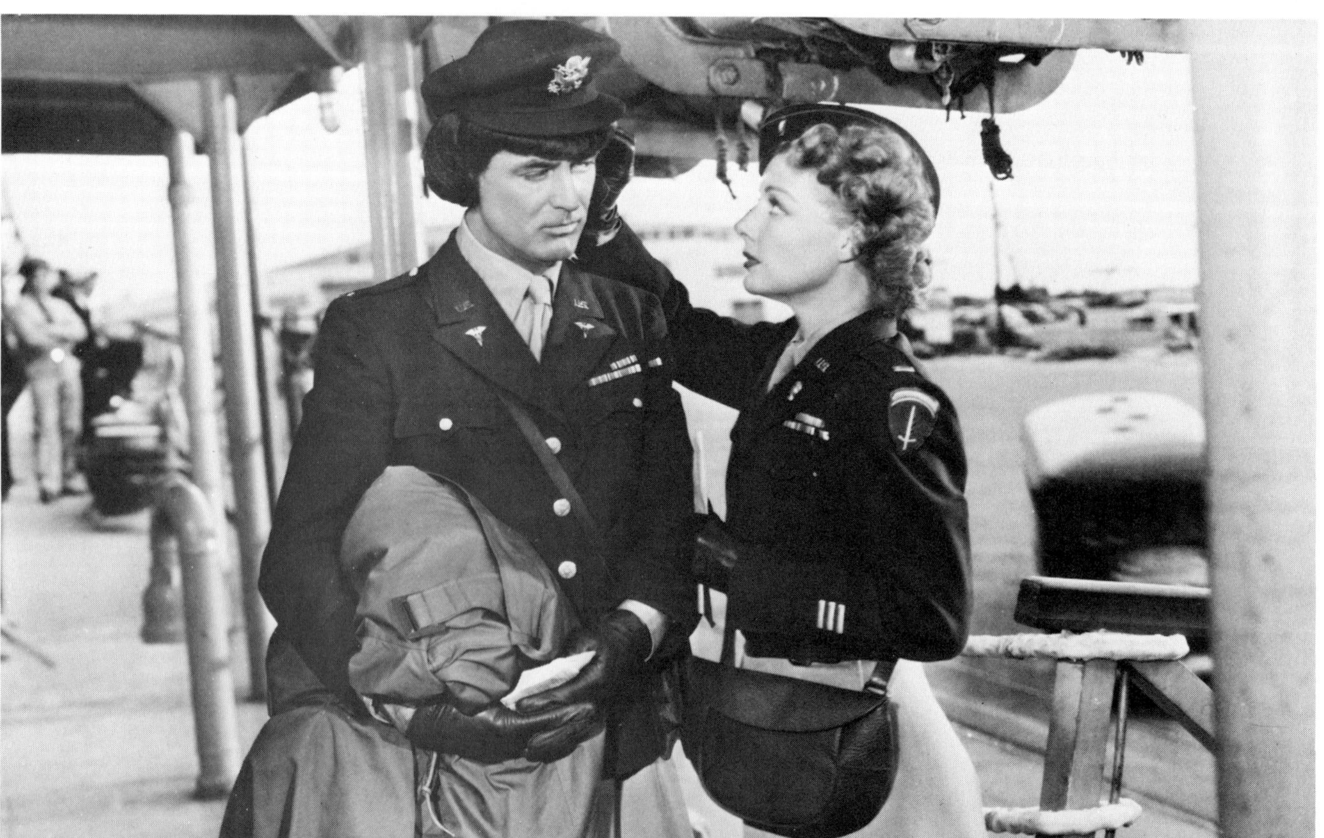

Paula Raymond and Gilbert Roland (r.) in *Crisis* (1950).

(Above left) With Betsy Drake in *Every Girl Should Be Married* (1948).

(Left) With Ann Sheridan in *I Was A Male War Bride* (1949).

1948 **EVERY GIRL SHOULD BE MARRIED** (RKO). Director, Don Hartman. Cast included: Eddie Albert, Betsy Drake, Alan Mowbray, Franchot Tone, and Elisabeth Risdon. Screenplay, Don Hartman and Stephen Morehouse Avery; based on a story by Eleanor Harris.

1949 **I WAS A MALE WAR BRIDE** (Twentieth Century-Fox). Director, Howard Hawks. Cast included: Eugene Gericke, Marion Marshall, William Neff, Ann Sheridan, and Randy Stuart. Screenplay, Charles Lederer, Leonard Spigelgass, and Hagar Wilde; from a story by Henri Rochard.

1950 **CRISIS** (MGM). Director, Richard Brooks. Cast included: Leon Ames, Teresa Celli, Jose Ferrer, Signe Hasso, Antonio Moreno, Ramon Navarro, Paula Raymond, and Gilbert Roland. Screenplay, Richard Brooks; based on a story by George Tabori.

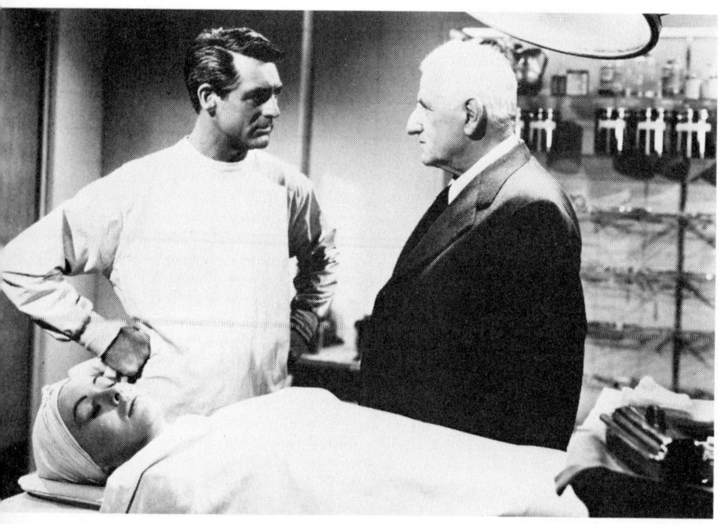

1951 **PEOPLE WILL TALK** (Twentieth Century-Fox). Director, Joseph L. Mankiewicz. Cast included: Sidney Blackmer, Jeanne Crain, Hume Cronyn, Finlay Currie, Margaret Hamilton, Katherine Locke, Walter Slezak, and Will Wright. Screenplay, Joseph L. Mankiewicz; adapted from a play by Curt Goetz.

1952 **ROOM FOR ONE MORE** (Warner Bros.). Director, Norman Taurog. Cast included: Malcolm Cassell, Betsy Drake, Gay Gordon, Iris Mann, Larry Olsen, Clifford Tatum, Jr., Lurene Tuttle, and George Winslow. Screenplay, Jack Rose and Melville Shavelson; from a book by Anna Perrott Rose.

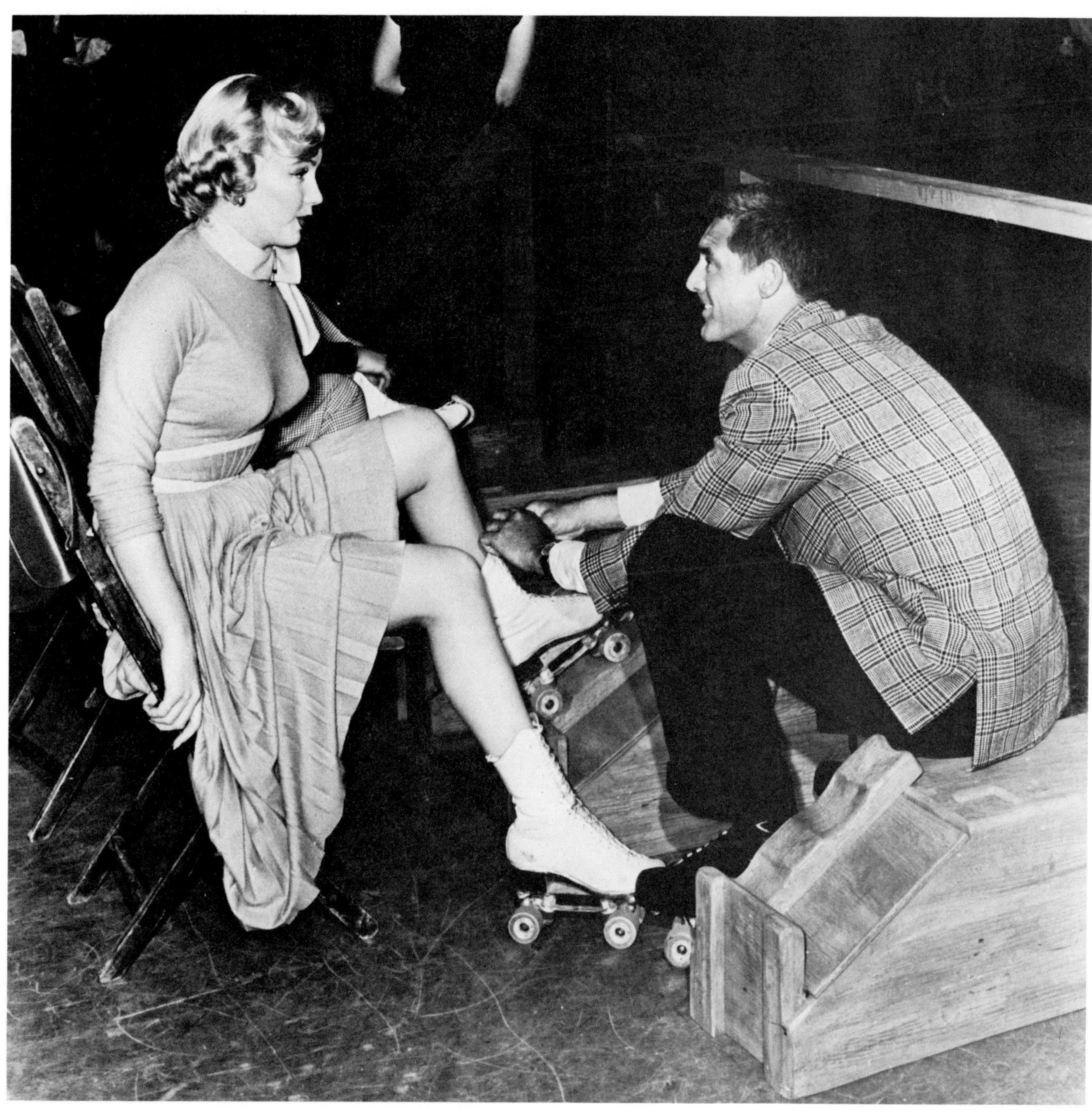

With Marilyn Monroe in *Monkey Business* (1952).

(Above left) With Jeanne Crain and Finlay Currie (r.) in *People Will Talk* (1951).

(Left) With Besty Drake in *Room for One More* (1952).

1952 **MONKEY BUSINESS** (Twentieth Century-Fox). Director, Howard Hawks. Cast included: Charles Coburn, Esther Dale, Henri Letondale, Larry Keating, Hugh Marlowe, Marilyn Monroe, Ginger Rogers, and George Winslow. Screenplay, I.A.L. Diamond, Ben Hecht, and Charles Lederer.

With Deborah Kerr (l.), Buddy Baer, and Betta St. John (r.) in *Dream Wife* (1953).

With Frank Sinatra (c.) and Sophia Loren in *The Pride And The Passion* (1957).

1953 **DREAM WIFE** (MGM). Director, Sidney Sheldon. Cast included: Buddy Baer, Bruce Bennett, Eduard Franz, Deborah Kerr, Walter Pidgeon, Betta St. John, and Les Tremayne. Screenplay, Herbert Baker, Alfred Lewis Levitt, and Sidney Sheldon.

1955 **TO CATCH A THIEF** (Paramount). Director, Alfred Hitchcock. Cast included: Bridgett Auber, Grace Kelly, Jessie Royce Landis, Jean Martinelli, Charles Vanel, and John Williams. Screenplay, John Michael Hayes; taken from the novel by David Dodge.

(Above) With Grace Kelly in *To Catch A Thief* (1955).

(Below) With Deborah Kerr in *An Affair To Remember* (1957).

1957 **THE PRIDE AND THE PASSION** (United Artists). Director, Stanley Kramer. Cast included: Theodore Bikel, Sophia Loren, Jay Novello, Frank Sinatra, and John Wengraf. Screenplay, Edna and Edward Anhalt; based on a novel by C.S. Forester.

1957 **AN AFFAIR TO REMEMBER** (Twentieth Century-Fox). Director, Leo McCarey. Cast included: Richard Denning, Deborah Kerr, Robert Q. Lewis, Cathleen Nesbitt, and Neva Patterson. Screenplay, Delmer Daves and Leo McCarey; from an original story by Mildred Cram and Leo McCarey.

With Suzy Parker (c.) and Jayne Mansfield (r.) in *Kiss Them For Me* (1957).

1957 **KISS THEM FOR ME** (Twentieth Century-Fox). Director, Stanley Donen. Cast included: Larry Blyden, Leif Erickson, Nathaniel Frey, Werner Klemperer, Jayne Mansfield, Jack Mullaney, Suzy Parker, and Ray Walston. Screenplay, Julius J. Epstein; adapted from a play by Luther Davis and a novel by Frederic Wakeman.

(Above right) With Ingrid Bergman in *Indiscreet* (1958).

(Right) With Sophia Loren (c.), Charles Herbert (l.), Paul Peterson (c.), and Mimi Gibson (r.) in *Houseboat* (1958).

1958 **INDISCREET** (Warner Bros.). Director, Stanley Donen. Cast included: Ingrid Bergman, Phyllis Calvert, Megs Jenkins, Oliver Johnston, David Kossoff, and Cecil Parker. Screenplay, Norman Krasna; from a play by Krasna.

1958 **HOUSEBOAT** (Paramount). Director, Melville Shavelson. Cast included: Eduardo Ciannelli, Mimi Gibson, Harry Guardino, Murray Hamilton, Charles Herbert, Martha Hyer, Sophia Loren, and Paul Petersen. Screenplay, Jack Rose and Melville Shavelson.

With James Mason (c.) and Eva Marie Saint in *North By Northwest* (1959).

(Left) With Joan O'Brien in *Operation Petticoat* (1959).

1959 **NORTH BY NORTHWEST** (MGM). Director, Alfred Hitchcock. Cast included: Leo G. Carroll, Josephine Hutchinson, Martin Landau, Jessie Royce Landis, James Mason, Edward Platt, Philip Ober, Eva Marie Saint, and Adam Williams. Screenplay, Ernest Lehman.

1959 **OPERATION PETTICOAT** (Universal). Director, Blake Edwards. Cast included: Tony Curtis, Gene Evans, Virginia Gregg, Dina Merrill, Joan O'Brien, Arthur O'Connell, Richard Sargent, and Robert F. Simon. Screenplay, Maurice Richlin and Stanley Shapiro; from a story by Paul King and Joseph Stone.

With Moray Watson (l.) and Robert Mitchum (c.) in *The Grass Is Greener* (1960).

(Right) With Doris Day in *That Touch Of Mink* (1962).

1960 **THE GRASS IS GREENER** (Universal). Director, Stanley Donen. Cast included: Deborah Kerr, Robert Mitchum, Jean Simmons, and Moray Watson. Screenplay, Hugh and Margaret Williams; based on their play.

1962 **THAT TOUCH OF MINK** (Universal). Director, Delbert Mann. Cast included: John Astin, Doris Day, Joey Faye, Alan Hewitt, Audrey Meadows, Richard Sargent, and Gig Young. Screenplay, Nate Monaster and Stanley Shapiro.

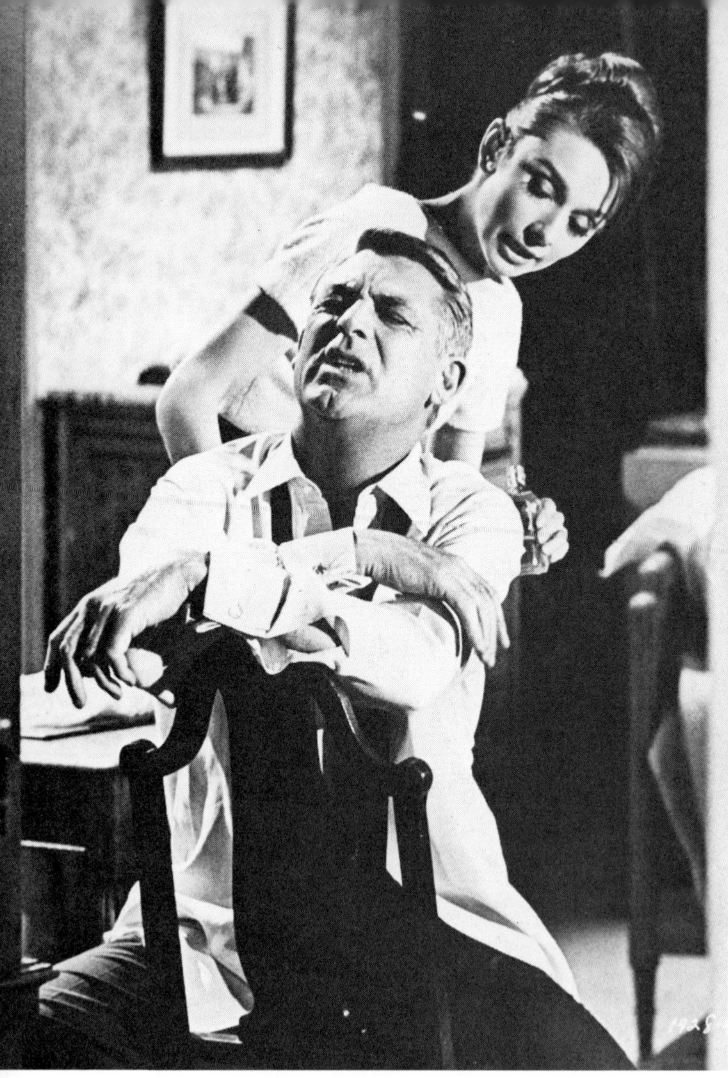

With Audrey Hepburn in *Charade* (1963).

1963 **CHARADE** (Universal). Director, Stanley Donen. Cast included: James Coburn, Ned Glass, Audrey Hepburn, George Kennedy, Jacques Marin, and Walter Matthau. Screenplay, Marc Behm and Peter Stone.

1964 **FATHER GOOSE** (Universal). Director, Ralph Nelson. Cast included: Jennifer Berrington, Stephanie Berrington, Leslie Caron, Jack Good, and Trevor Howard. Screenplay, Peter Stone and Frank Tarloff; adapted from a story by S.H. Barnett.

1966 **WALK, DON'T RUN** (Columbia). Director, Charles Walters. Cast included: Samantha Eggar, Ted Hartley, Jim Hutton, John Standing, and Miiko Taka. Screenplay, Sol Saks; based on a story by Frank Ross and Robert Russell.

(Right) With Jim Hutton (l.) in *Walk, Don't Run* (1966).

With Leslie Caron in *Father Goose* (1964).